BON JOVI

BON JOVI

WHEN WE WERE BEAUTIFUL

CONVERSATIONS WITH PHIL GRIFFIN

COLLINS DESIGN

An Imprint of HarperCollinsPublishers

WHEN YOU HAVE A SONG
THAT BECOMES A PART OF PEOPLE'S LIVES,
FOREVER MARKING MEMORIES,
IT'S NOTHING SHORT OF MAGIC.
IT'S THE CLOSEST THING TO IMMORTALITY
WE'LL EVER KNOW.
—JON

INTRODUCTION

BY PHIL GRIFFIN

It's cold in Minnesota. It's February 2007, a drafty hotel room, a tour-weary rock star and a somewhat juvenile British photographer. The guy behind the lens just wants to take a portrait. As with all life studies, you hope to capture the truth of the man. It's different if the subject happens to have endured a million clicks and flashes over twenty-five years at the top of his game. I can't help thinking it's the last thing Jon Bon Jovi wants to do right now.

But ever the professional, Jon endured. Looking back to where this all began, it's funny how one photograph, a stolen moment really, touched a nerve, inspired faith, and created an understanding between us. With that one image, never planned but always hoped for, Bon Jovi and I began a journey—a journey that has been inspiring, exciting, exhausting, and, at times, frustrating. Lets face it: You don't simply go on the road with one of the biggest bands in the world and expect to be given free rein. Or do you?

The joke out on the tour was always that whenever I had my camera in my hand, I somehow slipped into an invisible cloak—like some lens-toting Frodo Baggins with his magic ring. For whatever reason, Jon just didn't see me, Richie simply smiled, Tico winked, and Dave snarled his best keyboard king snarl.

It is the willingness of Jon, Richie, Tico, and Dave to let me in, let me be there, and let me take these pictures that has created the new material for this book. It is exciting for me to see the new and old share these pages. I hope it offers both a new perspective and a proud record of the past. It is, of course, both an honor and a responsibility, and I am doubly grateful that my pictures sit alongside the iconic images by Olaf Heine, Cynthia Levine, Mark Weiss, and all of the contributors to this anthology.

After our long trek on the Bon Jovi trail, making this book has taught me why this band is what it is. Why they have endured, why they are loved. It's simple, really; they are a family.

Jon is a complicated fellow. Watching him as I have had to do has felt a little bit like spying on your brother. Not always comfortable, but a guilty pleasure nonetheless. It is Jon's tireless drive and complexity that create such a perfect foil for Richie's infectious enthusiasm. To my mind, this is what makes these guys such great partners. I am proud to have been let into just a small part of that very private brotherhood.

Watching this band thru a lens has been a great way of focusing on where their trust in each other was born. To me it comes from the avenues and alleyways of Jersey, in the bars and clubs of the neighborhoods of their youth. It's in the fabric of the walls in Jon's studio on the banks of the Navesink River. It's in the strings of Richie's guitars and in the backbone of Tico's godfather-like presence at the back of the stage. These guys, much misunderstood but always steadfast in their identity, knew what their bottom line was—trust each other, tight-fist the world, and no one can break the circle.

I hope these pictures throw a light onto that truth. Each one has been chosen with care and pride. That's what these guys do to you: They make you care, make you want just a little bit of that brotherhood, a small slice of the family pie that is the Bon Jovi way.

Talking of bottom lines, for me a truly great picture is indeed a stolen moment, a piece of a soul that once taken can never be given back. I am proud that Jon and his band have trusted me enough to let me steal pieces of their hearts to share with you.

—Phil Griffin, 2009

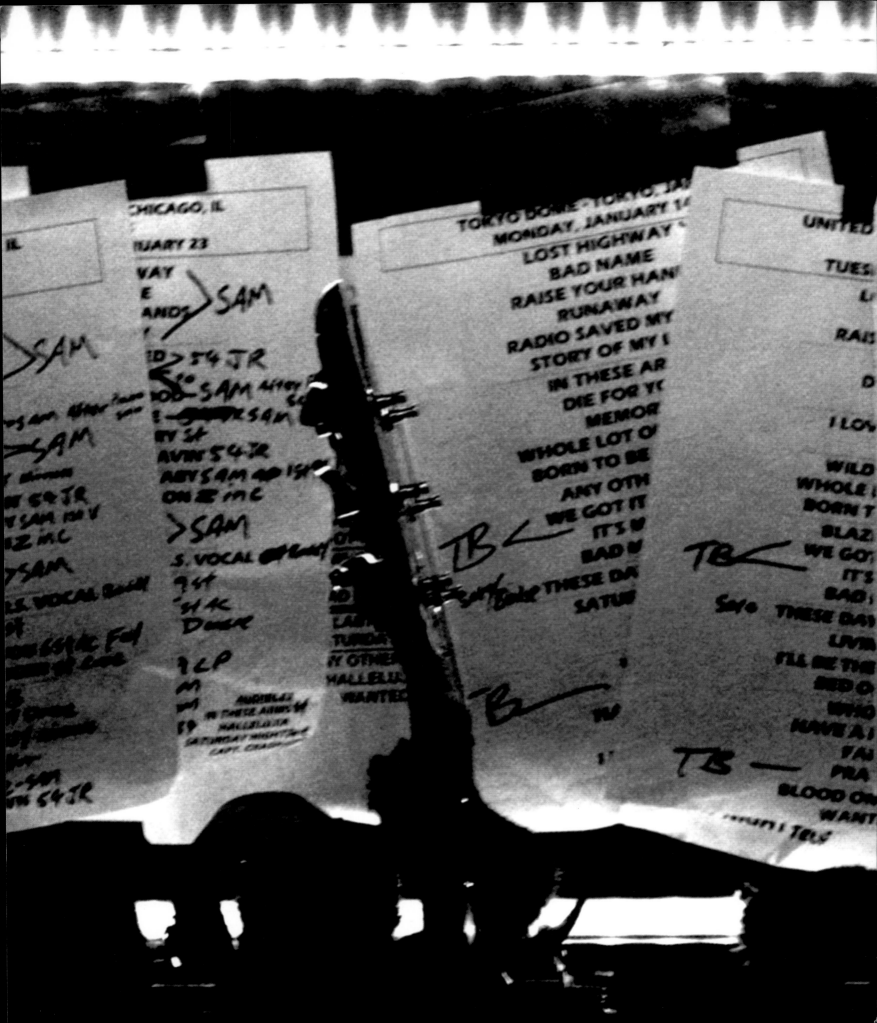

JON

As far as I'm concerned, the world began when Sinatra swooned, Presley swayed, the Beatles sang, "She Loves You," and the Stones flaunted their sympathetic vil-may-care swagger. The rest of it just sort of opened.

Since the beginning of the rock 'n' roll era, the a of being in, or around, a band gave you license to ill, if not the masses then yourselves.

In a band, you always felt invincible. Why? :ause you knew you were among brothers, nrades, gang members. And if you dared, if you ieved, you were Rock Stars.

Any successful musician will tell you it takes equal ts talent, sweat, and swagger to make up the magic mula. Sure, there are ups and downs at every level our career. But over time those ups and downs :ome memories, and as you look back on them (like old pictures your mother drags out at Christmas) all old hurts somehow feel better and the story seems hine brighter.

In any successful band, there has to be a lot of chemistry. Sinatra had Tommy Dorsey, then Nelson Riddle. Hell, he had the Rat Pack. Elvis had D. J. Fontana, Scotty Moore, then the Colonel and the Memphis Mafia. Paul had John, George, and Ringo. Mick had Keith and Charlie. Well, you get the idea. M— had Tico, I had David, and I had Richie.

For twenty-five years, Richie Sambora has been my right hand—the brother, partner, and friend you hope to one day find from the time when you're a kid. I tell people—and I mean this as the highest compliment—you would be lucky to call him your friend. He has the talent and desire that set him apart from the average guy slinging a six-string around. Sure, there are loads of guys who can play. There are lots of guys who can sing. But there is—and only ever will be—one Richie Sambora.

In any band, each member has a job to do. Tico Torres not only holds the bottom down sonically but has, for a long time, been the voice of reason—the elder statesman, if you will. He once said to me, "You know I love you. I've been watching your ass for the last twenty-five years." He has watched me guide this ship's course since its inception. He had the faith to leave a successful band with a recording contract for a kid, a garage, and a dream. I hope he thinks it was worth it. I'm sure glad he chose to come along.

David Bryan has played in bands with me, on and off, since I was sixteen. I remember his father had a van and he had a Hammond B3. Dave might have been seventeen when we first played together. I like to bust him because he's twenty-two days older than I am. He's old. He's also a very funny guy who has added his share of fun to our mix. Now he's a big shot on

PREVIOUS, PAGES 10-11: "Whole Lot of Leavin'" portrait session, Minneapolis, MN, March 17, 2008. OPPOSITE: *Lost Highway* tour, XCEL Energy Center, St. Paul, MN, March 2008 FOLLOWING, PAGES 14-15: *Lost Highway* tour, Twickenham Stadium, London, England, June 28, 2008.

Broadway, and of course he won't need us anymore. At least I can say, "I knew him when ..."

I felt a lot of reservations about doing this book and filming this movie. Why? Because I've always said our book isn't written yet. I may have been at this for a quarter of a century, but in a lot of ways I feel like we're just getting started. One thing we don't do around here is glide.

OK. I'll admit it. We actually enjoy what we do for a living. We make records. We sing for thousands of people every night. What's not to love? Each other? Maybe, some nights. But I'll tell you what. I can say something bad about one of my guys and that's OK. If you try it, I'll knock you out.

I'd like to thank so many people here on this page—like Paul Korzilius. P. K. has done everything as a manager that a client or friend could ever ask for. He doesn't know the meaning of the words "can't," "won't," or "no"—unless he has to say them to the promoter or record company. Sometimes I think he does it just for fun. There is a reason the *Lost Highway* tour was the biggest tour in the world for 2008: Paul Korzilius.

Hugh McDonald has played bass for me longer than there's been a Bon Jovi. He actually played on "Runaway" when I didn't have a band. He was the obvious and only choice to tour with the band after Alec John Such's departure in the mid-90s. It's Hugh and Tico's chemistry that makes us sound so good. And, truth be told, it's Hugh and Tico in my monitors every night. No need for much of anything else.

Jerry Edelstein is by trade an attorney, but to me he is a father, a brother, and the reason we are who and what we are. He is the Godfather—not only to my firstborn but to me. I wish any kid who starts in this business the blessing that you might find your own Godfather to protect you in this wicked world.

Jack Rovner took this vision and made it a reality. Every idea needs someone to implement it and make it better than it was when it was conceived. Jack did that. It has been his diligence that made this film and book possible. If he keeps opening doors for us, we're not shy, we'll walk right in.

And then there are the fans of the band. Every band says they owe it to their fans, but in our case it couldn't be more true. We didn't have the media on our side. We didn't have the machine. We had—and still have—*you*, the generation that came up with us and the generation you've passed our music on to. Thanks for giving me the opportunity to write this down, twenty-five years in—and counting.

—JBJ

BAND OF BROTHERS

PREVIOUS, PAGES 16–17: Outtake from *Bounce* photo shoot,
Ten 9 Fifty Studios, Culver City, CA, July 10, 2002. THIS PAGE,
ABOVE: Band photo shoot, The Eleanor, Long Island City, NY,
December 2, 2008; RIGHT: *Lost Highway* tour, end of show,
XCEL Energy Center, St. Paul, MN, March 2008.

JON: Why are we here at this point in our lives?

Because we have chosen this path. We've *chosen* to be here.

From the day I got into this, I wanted to write a song, and if you wrote a song and you felt it was a good song, you wanted to record it. If the recording came out as good as the piece of paper that you wrote it on, then you wanted to share it with as many people as possible.

I want to be out there because I want to see the reaction. I want to know that it touched you. I want to know that it touched your life. This is who we are. This is what we do and we do it well.

RICHIE: We are a real success story. If people learn our story, they'll get an insight into how we navigated our way through the music business and through our relationships within this band.

TICO: We are a tight fist and it works better that way. We're guarded, always have been. If you are going to tight fist the world as a musician, it's not about your being angry. We are going to do it together. We are going to fight and make it the best band, the best music, the best show possible.

People see us as a band of brothers. Sometimes we manage to connect onstage where you couldn't fit a sliver of paper between us.

JON: Everybody brings a lot to the table. There's no dividing line. Everyone's a shoulder to lean on; everybody's got a real, true opinion; everyone has shown each other how to grow, how to be responsible, be driven, be excitable, to have fun, and live in the moment.

TICO: That's the family side of Bon Jovi. There's a bubble, an insulation we have when we're together. We are a family and I think that does translate onstage.

PREVIOUS, PAGES 20–21: *Lost Highway* tour, end of show, XCEL Energy Center, St. Paul, MN, March 2008. OPPOSITE: *These Days* tour, the band's private plane, Cardiff International Airport, Cardiff, Wales, 1995. FOLLOWING, PAGES 24–25: *Lost Highway* tour, XCEL Energy Center, St. Paul, MN, March 2008.

THE
BEGINNING

JON: I think any kid who picks up a guitar should only ever think that he's going to be Mick Jagger—not "I want to be the opening act for Jagger." No. "I want to be Mick fucking Jagger." You should want to leave a legacy, move yourself, move people, leave a mark.

When you're young, you believe you can do something seemingly impossible, like make a record.

Jersey was in the shadows between Philadelphia and New York. It was suburbia, yet you had access to the worlds of art and theater, radio and television. It was incredible to live on the periphery of all that.

DAVID: New Jersey was a melting pot of opportunity.

JON: I grew up believing anything was possible. That was the American mindset in the early 60s, the Kennedy era of Camelot and space. The president told this country: "We're gonna go to the moon," and you believed him. I was born into that.

The great thing about being in Jersey was it was small enough that the impossible seemed possible. In the 70s, I didn't want to be in KISS or Led Zeppelin because those were too big, too fantastic to be real. But we had guys twenty miles away on the beach making records in our own backyard and I thought that was the big time. That's what I strived for.

DAVID: Jon knew that if you were a cover band, you would always be a cover band. If you were an original band, you'd make no money, but hopefully, one day, cover bands would be playing your songs.

When Jon was shopping "Runaway" around, my mother worked for Eastern Airlines and she got Jon and me tickets to California. We stayed in the Golden Lion Motel. We shopped "Runaway" in LA and were turned down. Then everybody in New York turned us down.

JON: "Runaway" finally being played in New York City—that's how we broke. There was no label. There was no promotion. There was no big manager.

I walked into WAPP, a new radio station, and played "Runaway" for the DJ. He liked it and WAPP put "Runaway" on their compilation album of local artists. WAPP played "Runaway" on the air in New York. Then their sister stations across the country started playing the song and the phones started lighting up. They were getting more requests for "Runaway" than for huge signed artists. All of a sudden, the record companies that said *no* said *yes*.

DAVID: Jon got a record deal and the band was formed around that. The deal was in Jon's name. Jon was signed to the label and we were signed to him. The cement was Jon. He always had that vision. He always saw the whole picture. As much as we were a band, he was the captain of the ship.

But it was everybody's efforts and everybody's sacrifice that really made it work. You knew then and there, from all the other players you'd played with, that you had to have a certain heart and a certain amount of determination to sacrifice everything to make it. You give up everything.

Tico was that guy. Richie was that guy. We said to family, friends, lovers, haters, anybody: I'm getting on the bus and I'm going to work my fucking ass off. And if I make it, I make it.

Early on, we'd get onstage and have to perform in front of some unfriendly, almost hostile, crowds. But by the end of our set, those guys were clapping and putting their fists up in the air. We got in your face and just by sheer will, we were going to win you over.

PREVIOUS, PAGES 26–27: Sanctuary Sound II, current Bon Jovi recording studio, Middletown, NJ, April 2009; PAGE 29, CLOCKWISE: Tico, 1975; Jon in Seaside Heights, NJ, summer 1980; Richie in childhood bedroom, Woodbridge, NJ, 1972; David and Richie, 1985. OPPOSITE, FROM TOP: *7800° Fahrenheit* tour, Jon in dressing room, Mississippi Coliseum, Jackson, MS, November 26, 1985; Jon onstage at Madison Square Garden for the first time, opening for ZZ Top, New York, NY, September 24, 1983; Richie working on Bon Jovi's debut album at The Power Station, New York, NY, July 1983.

TICO: You play a thousand clubs. You play in a hundred different bands and you learn. It's the cloth you are made of. It comes from long years of playing with everybody else and learning your craft. And a guy that doesn't wanna be there? You could feel it. You don't wanna play with them.

RICHIE: Jon's got that "thing," that charisma. First time I saw him, I said this guy's got "it."

JON: Our slogan at the time was "the best-kept secret in rock 'n' roll." We were that band you didn't want opening for you. We would do what Southside Johnny referred to as "head-hunting." You didn't want me opening for you, 'cause I'd do anything to upstage you. Anything. I'd come flying off the ceilings. I'd just do anything.

PREVIOUS, PAGE 32: *New Jersey* tour, 1989; PAGE 33: Jon in manager Doc McGhee's office, 1987. THIS PAGE, FROM TOP: Outside Knightsbridge tube station, London, England, August 1987; *New Jersey* tour, band huddle, Japan, 1989; St. Basil's Cathedral, Moscow, U.S.S.R., August 1989; OPPOSITE: Bon Jovi: (from left) Richie Sambora, Alec John Such, Jon Bon Jovi, Tico Torres, and David Bryan backstage, *New Jersey* tour, 1989.

THE
BIG
TIME

DAVID: The first time our tour bus pulled up, I was still living with my mom and dad. Richie and Jon were still living with their parents too. The bus pulled up and the neighbors came out with curlers in their hair going, "That's a tour bus?"

The first album went gold in Japan. That was huge! Then I came home sixty grand in debt because I had borrowed money for keyboards. That's when I learned the word "recoupable," which is worse than "fuck." In my house, my kids can say "fuck." If they say "recoupable," I wash their mouths out with soap.

So we had a gold record yet nothing. Then the second record didn't go platinum; we only sold 800,000 records …

JON: We were babies on the first record and the second one was done nine months later.

DAVID: At that point it was do or die. The third album, if it didn't break big, we were done. We were actually luckier than today where you have to have a hit on the first record or you're over. At least we had a shot to try to develop into something.

TICO: I think every band goes through that in the beginning. It was nice to have the chance to find our voice.

JON: You can talk to people who were in positions of power and they'll say, "We gave you that third album." It was a different era. You could break out of Philly or Cleveland or Pittsburgh or Asbury Park, like Southside

Johnny. There were regional bands in America and one DJ could influence things. *If* he played your record, you could break regionally. In today's world, it would be very hard.

DAVID: The powers that be saw that we were a hardworking band. We played every one of our shows; we went to the radio stations; we did all the interviews; we didn't fuck off. We really worked. We were dedicated.

TICO: I've been a musician for forty years. Before Bon Jovi there were fifteen years I played with just as much heart and love. But we got lucky. There is a certain magic that works, and being in the right place at the right time made us the biggest band in the world.

JON: We made a bunch of videos and we hated them all. Our early videos sucked. I didn't understand the medium whatsoever. We were twenty-one years old. We didn't know any better. We were really uneducated. So first album, first video, second album, third video … we started having a little more fun by the fourth or fifth video. And by *Slippery*, we figured it out.

DAVID: What really worked best for us? Live. When we played live, we kicked ass. Our records had to have the energy of a live show, and our videos had to have the energy of a live show to work.

Slippery When Wet came together and all the planets and moons and stars lined up.

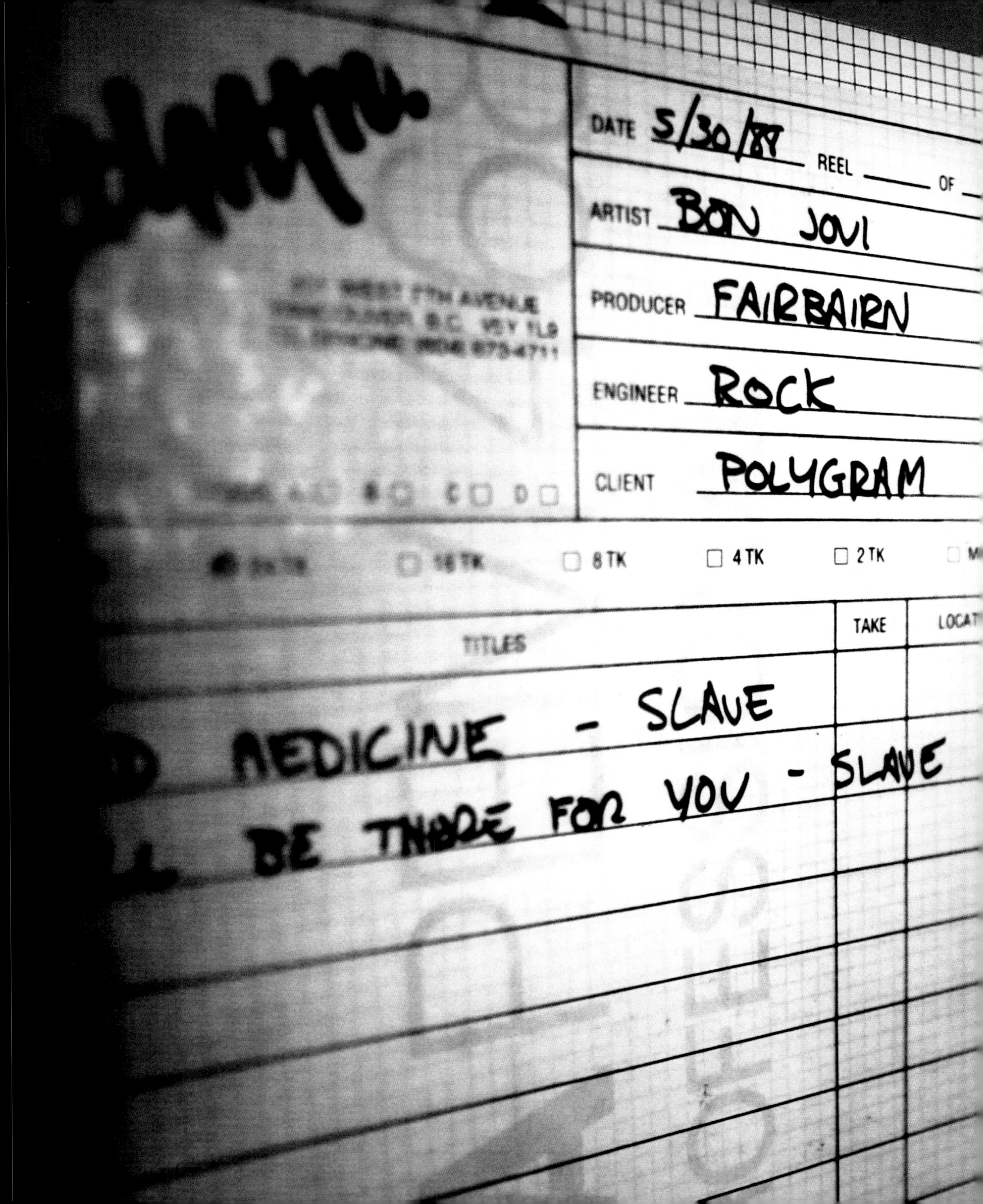
DATE 5/30/88
REEL
OF
ARTIST BON JOVI
PRODUCER FAIRBAIRN
ENGINEER ROCK
CLIENT POLYGRAM
8 TK
4 TK
2 TK
TITLES
TAKE
MEDICINE - SLAVE
BE THERE FOR YOU - SLAVE

DAVID: You have to bring it to the world. So we toured and toured and toured. We were never in the same place—always moving, always moving. As soon as we finished the huge *Slippery* tour, we recorded *New Jersey*, released it, and hit the road again. We worked ourselves to death. Between 1984 and 1990, I was home for six months. Six months in six years!

JON: We had nowhere else to go! What can be better than that? Compounded by the fact that you're young, you want to see the world, you're making money. And talk about everything being at your fingertips ... you name it. It was at our fingertips.

TICO: There was no family or kids. We were pretty much free. It made sense.

PREVIOUS, PAGES 36–37: *Lost Highway* tour, Punchestown Racecourse, Dublin, Ireland, June 7, 2008; PAGE 39: Jon and Richie, *New Jersey* tour, 1989; PAGES 40–41: Bon Jovi: (from left) David Bryan, Alec John Such, Jon Bon Jovi, Richie Sambora, and Tico Torres in a promotional photo shoot for the *Slippery When Wet* tour, Rumson, NJ, 1986. PAGES 42–43: Original slave/work reel for *New Jersey* album tracks, photographed at New Jersey archives, April 2009.

JON: With the *New Jersey* record, I refused to have anyone think all this was luck. We wanted to show that with the first two records there was something there, and even though the third one did pay off—big time—I was going to keep fighting to make sure you knew I could do this again and again and again. We weren't going to be a one-hit wonder.

There was a moment in time when we could have done anything, anywhere and gotten away with it.

DAVID: It wasn't as if we'd changed. It felt like one week nobody gave a shit about us and the next week we're the biggest thing on the planet. We looked the same. We played the same songs. We had the same intensity. But the world all of a sudden viewed us differently.

RICHIE: I think I definitely understood the success. It was massive. You know that you've made a dent, a big one, as an artist. Jon and I really came into our own as songwriters during the *Slippery When Wet* and *New Jersey* period.

PREVIOUS, PAGE 44: Jon Bon Jovi, *These Days* tour, 1995; PAGE 45: Richie Sambora, *One Wild Night* tour, The Schott, Columbus, OH, May 4, 2001. THIS PAGE, LEFT: David Bryan, *These Days* tour, 1995; RIGHT: Tico Torres, *One Wild Night* tour, Europe, Summer 2001; OPPOSITE: Bon Jovi: (from left) Alec John Such, David Bryan, Richie Sambora, Jon Bon Jovi, and Tico Torres, *Keep The Faith* tour plane, 1993.

DAVID: I think the touring brought us closer together. Living, coexisting, we really became a family. We spent more hours together than with any other person in our lives—wives, girlfriends, friends, parents. We were there every day for each other. Backstage and onstage, we were a team. Offstage too. We made sure nobody was getting into too much trouble. We covered each other's backs but some of us were really getting burned out.

TICO: There was a lot of touring. The touring was almost senseless, to the point where you didn't know where you were or why you were doing it anymore. It became a machine, which was well oiled, but you forgot why you were out there anymore. We never really sat for a minute and really enjoyed the success. We were part of that machine, which, at one point, was almost the demise of the band.

DAVID: Some people hold it together. Some people fall apart. Everybody had their own little mess going on. And it was more for some. Some was substances, some was life, and it just got out of hand. It just kept going and going and going and going. There had to be a breaking point. There just had to.

Jon is an insane workaholic. As much as he hates to do it, he loves to do it. Jon began hating something he loved, yet he kept pushing it. He could have said, "No. I don't want to do more." You keep grinding because you don't want it to end. Then you're exhausted. It got to the point where the only way Jon could sing was if he got a steroid shot. We'd gotten to the point where it was past the fun. And Jon's the guy, if he's not having fun … it doesn't work.

It stopped being fun for Jon probably more than for the rest of us. He wasn't a star. Then all of a sudden, he's a star. He had a lot more pressures.

He was a unique situation: You're the star. The focus; everything lands on you. But that's Jon's world. He's a complicated dude. Jon became introverted all of a sudden.

TICO: It was almost over. The band was completely overworked.

PAGES 48–49: Contact sheet of unapproved photos taken in Moscow, U.S.S.R., February 1989. FOLLOWING, PAGE 50: *Lost Highway* tour, XCEL Energy Center, St. Paul, MN, March, 2008; PAGE 53: Reviewing CD artwork for *One Wild Night: Live 1984–2001*, Los Angeles, CA, March 19, 2001.

RICHIE: Management came to us and said, "Do you wanna do another seventy shows?" And we went, "We gotta stop, man." That decision was a crucial point in the band's career.

We were just a mess—emotionally, physically. Life had changed drastically from three years prior. And in that three years' window, we were in the cocoon of a tour. Trying to fit back into life after that was the tricky part, I think.

Everybody was going through growing pains.

JON: Every other hour of every single day was spent together. We vacationed together. We didn't have houses so we'd live in hotels together. It will drain you 'cause, in a weird way, it's a sexless marriage. And it's family, but it's not. So you get to that crossroads and you burn out like we did.

TICO: On the last day of the *New Jersey* tour, we did two stadium shows in Guadalajara, Mexico. One was a matinee! Then we each got on different planes and flew home—and didn't talk for months and months and months.

RICHIE: I never really believed it was over. Something in my spirit inherently knew this wasn't the end for us.

I think that everybody interpreted the fame and fortune on different levels and at different speeds. We didn't understand what was happening but what I did know was this wasn't over. I never doubted that.

There was a lot that needed to be straightened out. There was business stuff that needed to be straightened out. There was the emotional thing that needed to be straightened out. There were ill feelings against each other because management would be talking to Jonny and telling him one thing, then selling me something else.

> THE TOURING WAS ALMOST SENSELESS, TO THE POINT WHERE YOU DIDN'T KNOW WHERE YOU WERE OR WHY YOU WERE DOING IT ANYMORE.
> —TICO

Jon was figuring out his own stuff … I always knew that we'd come to grips somehow … I didn't know when or how, but I knew that.…

DAVID: The band just went dormant. I got a nasty parasite from South America. It ate out my stomach lining, my intestines, and attacked my nerve endings. It was in my bloodstream; I was poisoned. I was 145 pounds, and I was really ill in the hospital for two weeks, then bedridden at home for a month … So my plight was a little different. The guys were all worrying about the band. I wasn't really worried about a job. I was worried about trying to stay alive.

RICHIE: You had five guys off on their own tangents. Jon and I did solo records.

Me doing that solo album, grabbing the guys, keeping that little piece of us employed was my effort to keep that part of the band together.

DAVID: Finally, Jon sat us down in a band meeting. He said, "I'm putting it all back together." He told us he was firing Doc, our manager. "I'm going to guide this vision," he said. "I believe we can do it." First, he hired a shrink.

TICO: It was Jon's idea. He found out about this guy and sought him out. I don't know how he did it. To me, it was a sign of brilliance to be able to call somebody who could help us.

JON: Lou Cox had no connection to the band. He came in and got us to speak better than anyone else could have because he didn't have an ulterior motive.

DAVID: I said, "I don't need no fucking shrink. That's for sick people. There's nothing wrong with me; there's something wrong with you." But everybody said, "Nothing wrong with me; something's wrong with you."

Lou Cox was a great thing. He got us to communicate. As much as you thought you were fucked up, everybody was. He really helped you to learn to say the things that you couldn't say before, but in a safe place. That kept us connected. It really helped us to just be honest enough to go on and move forward. It was the end of the beginning and the start of the new.

TICO: Lou Cox helped us a lot, as a group, to be able to deal with each other. He was a saving grace. That was our big secret for years and years.

DAVID: *Keep The Faith* represented what we'd survived. All of us said, "We're in this together. We are controlling our own destiny. Good or bad, we're gonna do it." We believed in Jon and his vision.

JON: By 1992, I can honestly say the drama was over. Everybody understood the future.

THE
VISION

JON: My wife says about anything I dare to do: "Will. You just will it to happen." I just kick and kick and kick … until it happens.

It's the rebellion in you that says, "I can, I will, and it's just a matter of when."

Whatever you want, you can do. Whatever you need to do, you'll get it done. That silly blind faith has pulled me through my life, no matter what it was …

RICHIE: I don't think critics care about the human side of what this organization represents.

JON: When you are that commercially successful, as we've been for as long as we've been, people want to hit you in the nose. That's just human nature.

DAVID: You're always fighting. When you actually make it to the top, you go, "OK, I did it." But in the back of your mind you're asking yourself, "Can I do it again?" That's Jon's world. Can you do it again? I said to Jon, "You're the kind of guy that has a chip on his shoulder. You have a battery on your shoulder, like that commercial. Knock it off. Knock this battery off my shoulder. I dare ya."

JON: We didn't become who we are today because we were lucky. We became this big because we're fucking pounding and pounding and punching and punching and punching—still.

DAVID: I'm not a shrink, but Jon's the kind of guy who uses that as one of his motivators. That's one of my motivators. I think for all of us in the band, it's our motivation. Everybody said, "You can't." I think if the critics said, "Wow, they're great," maybe we wouldn't fight as hard. Jon's the kind of guy who just has to prove himself every day. That's his deal with the devil. He has to prove everybody wrong.

JON: To tell you the honest-to-God truth, if we had had everybody patting us on the back for the last twenty years I'd have gotten fat and old and lazy; it would had been a lot easier than keeping the chip on your shoulder and going, "Gotta fight, gotta fight." But that's sort of motivational. I find it to be the reason you wake up in the morning.

RICHIE: Jon saddles himself with lots of responsibility. He loves that, thrives on it. That's basically where he comes from, I think. I've never seen anybody do it better than him. And it's not luck. It comes from thinking about it. It's the result of lots of trial and error in his mind. He's more intense than I am—for sure.

TICO: Each of us is a cogwheel in the clock. It's Jon's band and he's the leader. And he's a good leader and he's strong, but he's a multitasker and there are certain things that get by him as a human being. It's only natural.

TICO: Even though Jon wears the managerial hat, there's always somebody helping him. It's the same with the band. You could lean on the other guys. We've leaned on each other when we've had physical ailments, when we had issues with family, divorce, illness. You have to lean on each other.

DAVID: I'm around to tell jokes. I help Jon to get some levity in his world. I always said Jon was born with a horseshoe jammed in his ass and I'm holding on to it tight. Every once in a while I get a little shit on me. Who cares? Brush it off. We're still going. That guy made a deal with the devil. Definitely the devil. Well, maybe. There's good in evil.

JON: The truth of the matter is, like a football team, somebody has to be the quarterback. The quarterback can't win without a line to protect him. It's a team effort. It's the Henry Ford theory of management. Somebody's name has to be on the top and be the ultimate decision maker. True, it isn't a democracy but it is a team effort.

PREVIOUS, PAGES 54–55: Promotional portrait session, backstage, The Palace of Auburn Hills, Auburn Hills, MI, July 7, 2009; PAGE 56 (ALL): *Lost Highway* tour, hotel suite on day off, Marbella, Spain, June 2008. OPPOSITE: Sanctuary Sound II, Middletown, NJ, April 2009. FOLLOWING, PAGE 60 (ALL): Hell's Kitchen, New York, NY, December 8, 1999; PAGE 61: The Shoe Inn, Middletown, NJ, December 10, 1999.

DADDY DOESN'T KNOW BEST.
I LEARN BY TRIAL AND ERROR.
I SCREW UP AS MUCH AS,
OR MORE THAN, ANYONE ELSE DOES,
BUT I'VE HAD A VISION AND
THAT VISION SEEMS TO WORK.
—JON

SHOULDER
TO
SHOULDER

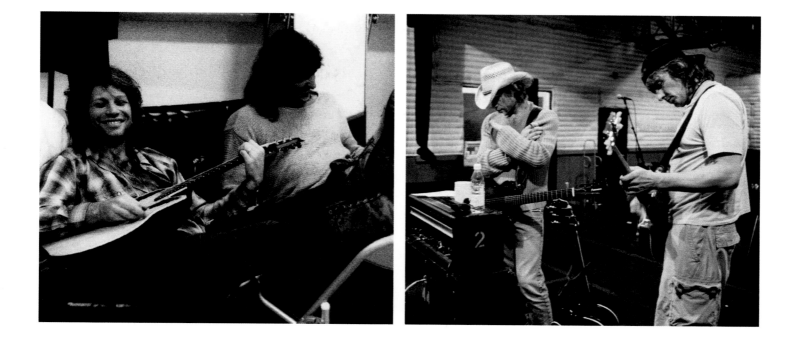

RICHIE: My journey has been steadfast: to be Jon's right-hand man. First and foremost, I try to always be there for him, as a friend, on a musical level, and from a business standpoint where he can use me as a mirror for himself.

We've always looked to Frank and Dean. Frank was the Chairman and Dean was the right-hand man. That's the way it was. It was a dynamic duo.

JON: One of my few regrets is never having met Frank Sinatra. When you read the obituaries, the articles, and the books—and you hear the songs—you start to really realize what he stood for. That made such an impact on me. What he stood for in the civil rights movement—walking in the front door with Sammy in Vegas. What he did when he was at his lowest. He didn't have a record deal, didn't have a movie deal. That's when he won the Academy Award. He ended up owning the record company. He put his guys together and created

the Rat Pack for what was supposed to be a couple of years of fun and it changed the world.

He got a president elected, for God's sake!

He fought for respect and he ultimately won it. He had the respect of his friends, his fans, his people. Yet he always had a chip on his shoulder.

But he could hang with princes and he could hang with paupers, and I like that about him. The guy was down and out but he kept coming back. He could have been just a teeny bopper idol. But ultimately, he became a king and he was always confident in who he was. Frank knew what he was, he knew what he did, and knew how to do it well. I thought that was pretty cool.

My mom got to meet Sinatra a few times when she was a Playboy Bunny. After I was making records, she went backstage at a Sinatra concert. She reintroduced herself to him and he made small talk about her kid, the singer from Jersey. She'd taken a *Rolling Stone* magazine with me on the cover and he signed it to me.

PREVIOUS, PAGES 62–63: *Lost Highway* tour, XCEL Energy Center, St. Paul, MN, March 2008. OPPOSITE: *Slippery When Wet* tour, 1986. THIS PAGE, LEFT: *These Days* tour, backstage, 1995; RIGHT: Rehearsal for *One Wild Night* tour, SIR Studios, Los Angeles, CA, March 18, 2001. FOLLOWING, PAGE 67, FROM TOP: Snakeskin jacket in Richie's quick-change tent; Dean Martin image in Richie's quick-change tent; Frank Sinatra image in Jon's quick-change tent. All three photos taken on *Lost Highway* tour, 2008.

I was like, "Oh, that's nice, Mom." Of course now I would have wanted to sit there for hours peppering him with questions. Especially, why'd you stay so loyal to those guys? I just love the idea of what he stood for.

Richie fits into the Dean role because he's been the comic relief, but also the voice of reason. He would always be that shoulder I could lean on. In a partnership, writing a song, or as your pal, he's the guy who has your back. If anyone were to ever say anything, Richie would be the first one to jump into the fray and punch him in the nose.

I liked how those guys supported each other throughout. But everyone knew Frank was the boss. He was the Chairman.

It seems to work in our little organization. It's fascinating because if you consider our peer group when we broke big, it certainly wasn't anything to latch onto. My peer group wouldn't have known what the Rat Pack was, yet we just naturally fell into that model.

Dave gets to be there for the comic relief, the Sammy kind of brunt of the joke where he knows no one's laughing at him. They're laughing with him. Richie gets to play the character of Dino, though Tico's really the guy who goes to bed early now.

RICHIE: Part of what I do and what I've always done, consciously, is really try to bring a good feeling to the organization. I'm not a guy who is shy about saying, "Hey, I love you," and giving you a hug.

If I can help Jon be in a great mood as much as possible, I'm going to do it. And that's the responsibility I put on myself and the guys too. I always felt that I gave good band.

Taking care of the guys was part of my gig and it started to fall apart a little bit when I was broken and I couldn't do it. I couldn't fulfill that responsibility to myself and the guys anymore. And that's when they started to realize they needed to pick me up. And they

WE'VE ALWAYS LOOKED TO FRANK AND DEAN.
—RICHIE

did. With the shit that I've been go
life over the past couple of years, t
paid back by my mates.

They are looking after me now.
of the wreckage. Just because you're
it does not make you exempt from li
And obviously, my life is so good, ho
up? How did I get tripped up? How d
You're supposed to be a man and no
you're older, but that's false. That's b
mount up on you, those trials and tri
in your life, you need your best frien
you grounded. This is what this band
help. I think it was a bad need. If it w
the band, we'd all do it, together. Eve
forces. That's the secret of this band.

TICO: That's where the band come
each other. We try to watch each ot
way. It saved my life.

DAVID: Everybody knows now wh
when to make a move, when to star
"You're wrong." It's safe for us to b
with each other.

TICO: Amongst ourselves, someb
up the slack here, picks it up there;
it work.

RICHIE

MY DEAR FRIEND, MY RIGHT HAND, GUITAR PLAYER EXTRAORDINAIRE, THE CONSIGLIERE, RICHIE SAMBORA.

—JON

A few years back, we started writing a "proper" band biography. The publishers wanted a tell-all and we were determined to tell nothing. No one was saying a word so we scrapped the idea. But in a way, that says all you need to know about this band.

Through the movie and this book, we're finally inviting people to witness the relationships between the band members and also between the public and the songs Jon and I have written. The connection people feel to our songwriting is part of what has kept us relevant over so many years. I feel so privileged to be a part of the soundtrack of people's lives.

The relationship between Jon, Tico, David, and me is a very special bond. It began as we fought to build a career and navigate the ever-changing waters of the music business together. It grew as we each battled our mutual and personal angels and demons. At different times, we were there to pick each other up, lend an ear, or offer a shoulder to lean on. We've spent more time together than with our families and that definitively makes us a family.

I FEEL SO PRIVILEGED TO BE A PART OF THE SOUNDTRACK OF PEOPLE'S LIVES. —RICHIE

Jon and I find ourselves closer than ever now; it's an anomaly the record business has never seen before. That Mick and Keith thing? It was a power struggle that never happened to us. We're tighter now, after twenty-six years of brotherhood and friendship.

Every night I walk onto the stage, look over my shoulder, and see Tico and Dave. I'm proud as hell to know I'm playing with the best musicians, my brothers. Jon, in my opinion, on any given night is the best front man in the business. I have such mad respect and love for all my bandmates. It is truly an honor.

I feel an enormous responsibility to the band, and especially the fans who come to see us from city to city, country to country, and all over the world. Every night, I give 100 percent of my heart onstage. I'm grateful for that opportunity. I thank you.

I'm excited, not just about the new album but about the future of Bon Jovi. We plan to maintain the integrity and dignity of our songwriting and record-making process and the journey will continue, searching for the evolution of what the band will be.

— Richie

PREVIOUS, PAGES 74–75: *Lost Highway* tour, XCEL Energy Center, St. Paul, MN, March 2008. THIS PAGE: *One Wild Night* tour, The Schott, Columbus, OH, May 4, 2001. OPPOSITE: *Lost Highway* tour, Punchestown Racecourse, Dublin, Ireland, June 7, 2008. FOLLOWING, PAGES 78–79: *New Jersey* tour, 1989; 80–81: *Slippery When Wet* tour, 1987.

THE SONGS

JON: The best part of this whole process to me is writing the song, seeing it on a piece of paper.

Then the second phase is recording it and seeing if it came out as good as it was in theory. And then, of course, you want to tour it.

What I try to do—and I realize that I do this to a fault—is I try to find the optimism. I don't like to write the downer song. I have, but I don't typically because I want to use the moment for the people who are listening to find something to lift them up.

The recurring theme of eternal optimism seems to be my niche. I'm living there. I'm very, very comfortable in knowing that niche is mine. Bon Jovi have *our* thing.

Art is subjective. It shouldn't make my music any more important or less important than anyone else's. It is what it is.

TICO: It's magic. It starts from a creative process. Jon and Richie work with a little tape player and some guitars to make a song that works for all of us. If you had a couple of different guys in the band, it would sound totally different. It wouldn't, it couldn't be the same song.

JON: You *can* craft a song. But I've found that whenever we crafted a song, those songs didn't work. I'm not that good a craftsman to make it work so it's got to come from a real place.

It's not a conscious effort to write a hit song. It's a conscious effort to write a great song and if a "Livin' On A Prayer" or "Who Says You Can't Go Home" or "It's My Life" is born, you go, "I want the world to know that we've just knocked one out of the park!"

Sure, "Bad Medicine" sounds cute and "You Give Love A Bad Name" is tongue-in-cheek. You remember the lyric though, right?

When I was twenty-five, "Bad Name" was the shit. We were in the mall. We had that hair and those clothes. It was real. That was us, then. But I couldn't do that today. I don't think we could sit down to write "You Give Love A Bad Name" again. It would be crafting and it wouldn't resonate.

TICO: You can't manufacture. If you manufacture anything that has to do with creativity—art, music, anything—it won't work. It will be transparent. It won't be felt.

JON: It's too important that we continue to write songs that move people. I'm not going to follow whatever the trend happens to be at the moment. I have to be true to myself.

We have to be true to ourselves as songwriters and true to what Bon Jovi is about.

RICHIE: When it comes down to Jon and I writing a song, it's pure. We're not thinking about business. We've written specific songs earlier in our careers saying, "This is going to work in an arena" or "This will work in a stadium." They were specifically made to get the crowd ready, get everybody's dander up, and deliver the knockout punch.

For the most part, Jon and I have remained the same people and our friendship has grown tighter over the years. Anytime you write songs together, everybody's got their own individual experience and idea of what the song is about. They are often different for Jon and me but we meet in the middle on things. Different songs mean different things to him.

When I'm up onstage singing, sometimes I'm really thinking about my dad. Certain lyrics turn out to mean something different over time. Some stuff you

wrote in 1990, it comes back around when you are performing it now. Life boomerangs and fits into those lyrical strands we'd written about years before. It's like looking at your life through a rearview mirror. It becomes clearer as you get older.

Our lyrics speak to how people really live, what they feel. Those are our feelings but when we write a song, we write a lyric people connect with naturally.

JON: From a songwriting point of view, we grew up after the *New Jersey* album. By then, I had a hell of a lot more to say and we were more mature.

DAVID: Our songs don't preach. We're not hitting somebody with a hammer saying, "This is my point of view. This is my point of view." Our lyrics invite you in. This is a point of view for all of us.

JON: We were working on the *Keep The Faith* album when the riots broke out in LA. Rodney King got beat up in the streets and there was LA burning. That era was over. The 80s were done. We were up in Vancouver and we watched LA burning on television.

"Keep The Faith" was a reaction to what we'd witnessed but we intentionally did not get specific. Hopefully people will understand the power of the lyric and what inspired it but in a year—or ten—it still needs to resonate. You want things to be timeless and classic. You want things to be there forever. So, it's not catering to this generation … it's for all generations. So we hone the lyric. We universalize it.

PREVIOUS, PAGES 82–83: Sanctuary Sound II, Middletown,
NJ, April 2009; PAGE 85: Sanctuary Sound II, Middletown, NJ,
April 2009; PAGES 86–87: Sanctuary Sound II, Middletown,
NJ, April 2009. THIS PAGE: *New Jersey* promotional photo shoot,
Little Mountain Recording Studios, Vancouver, B.C., Canada,
1988. OPPOSITE: Recording session for *Young Guns II: Blaze
of Glory*, A&M Studios, Los Angeles, CA, 1990. FOLLOWING,
PAGES 90–91: *Lost Highway* Tour, pre-show walk to the stage,
XCEL Energy Center, St. Paul, MN, March 2008.

RICHIE: *Lost Highway* evolved. The idea was to go down to Nashville and try something different. We had a great window after "Who Says You Can't Go Home." I think a band that has been together as long as we have, any time there is a door open to evolution, give it a shot.

JON: It was totally a get-out-of-jail-free card. Just try it. Who knew?

TICO: Not having any pressure, man. We were having fun.

RICHIE: It was an opportunity to experiment. We're in a place, at this point in our career, where we don't have to worry. If we don't like something, we just don't put it out.

JON: *Lost Highway* was an introspective record because we took a look at ourselves and left ourselves open to scrutiny by sharing those situations and feelings beyond the four of us. It was a great growth record. We were in a place where we had something to write about and turn our lives into big, broad subject matter.

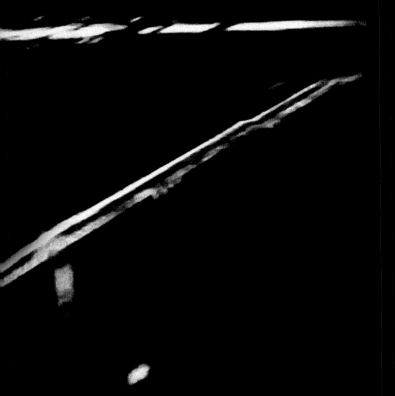

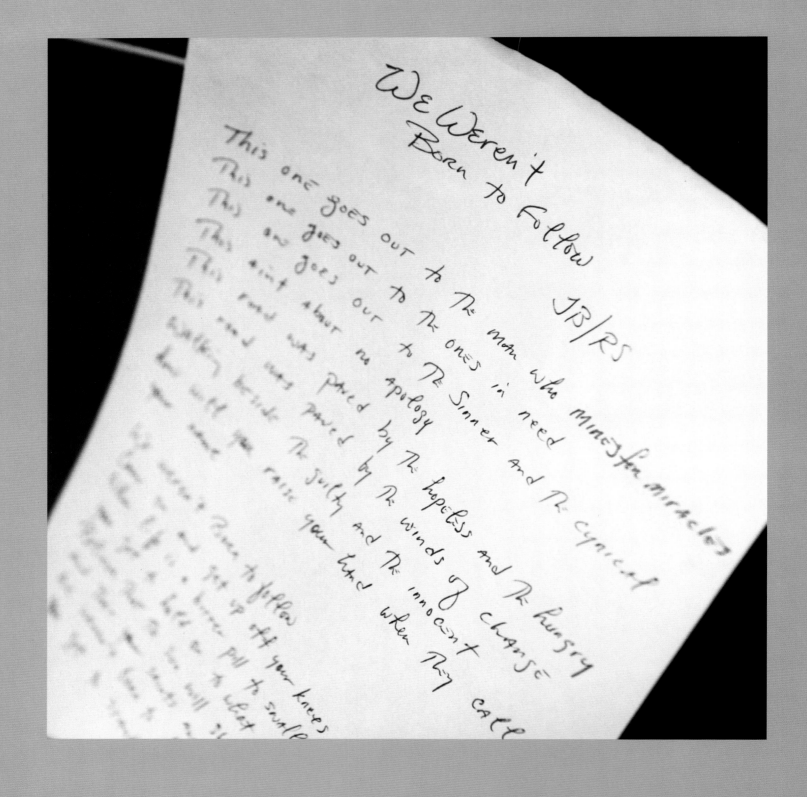

RICHIE: Everything we wrote about came from someplace real. The *Lost Highway* album represented what I was going through in my life, with substance abuse and emotions caused by my divorce and my father dying. It was cathartic. It's impossible, as an artist, for those feelings and emotions not to come through in your songs.

"Whole Lot Of Leavin'" was a song I didn't write, and Jon was still writing about me, I believe. I'm sure some of it was what was going on in his own life at the time.

When the fans get beneath the lyrics and read between the lines, they can feel that. A lot of fans have attached themselves to particular songs because they embrace the underlying meanings.

PREVIOUS, PAGE 92: Song lyrics handwritten by Jon Bon Jovi, photographed August 2009; PAGE 93: Sanctuary Sound II, Middletown, NJ, April 2009; PAGES 94–95: (BOTH) Sanctuary Sound II, Middletown, NJ, April 2009. OPPOSITE: Sanctuary Sound II, Middletown, NJ, April 2009.

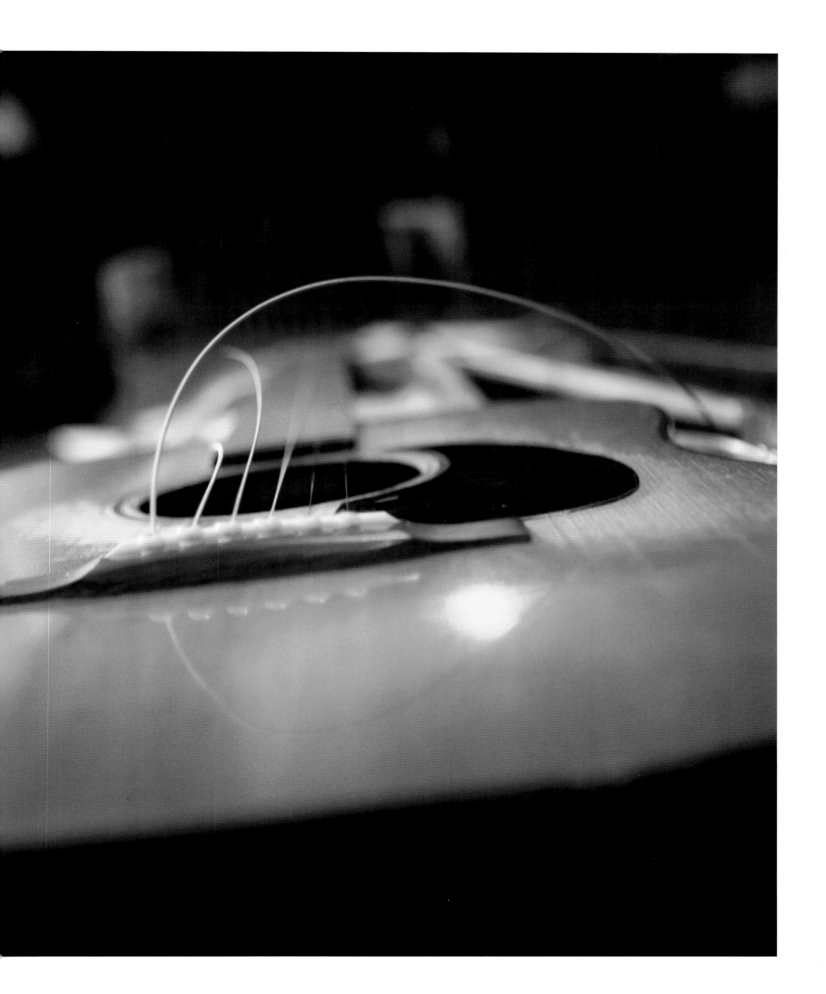

TICO

NO FIREWORKS,
THERE'S NO MUSIC.
—TICO

My musical journey has encompassed my life for over forty years. My creed, right from the beginning, was (and is) to communicate and speak through my instrument and keep myself open to all emotions and interaction.

Since the band got together twenty-five years ago, I believe the key to our longevity has been the common goal of pushing ourselves past our creative limits, not only in the studio but in our live performances. The key factor is our respect for each other's ability to push the envelope, individually and as a group.

It's been comforting to me to have my bandmates as friends and brothers during tough personal times and to share all our achievements together.

We are as good as our last record. That being said, we have never sat back on our accomplishments. Instead we strive to explore the unknown, yet always remember where we came from. Sure, we've weathered some tough storms but they only made us stronger. Music is full of wonderful accidents that will always take you to higher levels of creativity and success. That can continue forever, if we don't get in its way…

Simplicity is genius for us kids, and I never want to grow up.

—Tico

PREVIOUS, PAGES 98–99: *Lost Highway* tour, XCEL Energy Center, St. Paul, MN, March 2008. OPPOSITE: *Lost Highway* tour, soundcheck, Madison Square Garden, New York, NY, July 14, 2008. FOLLOWING, PAGES 102–103: *Lost Highway* tour, Punchestown Racecourse, Dublin, Ireland, June 7, 2008; PAGES 104–105: (ALL) Sanctuary Sound II, Middletown, NJ, April 2009.

DAVID

WE ONLY GROW STRONGER AS TIME GOES BY
—DAVID

What an amazing ride it's been for over twenty-five years! From the first time I met Jon in Sayreville in 1978 (when I was a mere seventeen years old) until today, the journey of this band has been an unbelievable series of events that have defined us.

I always knew the chemistry between us was undeniable; the combination is truly magical.

When you start out, you have dreams of making it *big time.* When we left New Jersey on our own tour bus for the first time, we were like Christopher Columbus, seeking new adventures in the great unknown.

I had the choice, as a young man, to become a surgeon or a classical pianist or join a rock 'n' roll band; I've always known my choice was correct. I've had the opportunity to bring music and joy to people around the planet (and had *a lot* of fun along the way). If you work hard and have a lot of luck, dreams can and do come true. I know that's a corny phrase ... until it happens to you.

Spending so much time together, fighting for the same cause, has cemented our relationships for good. We could never break up. We only grow stronger as time goes by. We've always had each other to rely on in good times (and not so good times). A band of brothers always watches each other's backs.

Thank you, Jon, Tico, and Richie, for making my life very special. Our lives have been an adventure few people get to experience. It always has been, is, and will be an honor, pleasure, and privilege to play alongside each of you, until I can't play any longer.

— David

PREVIOUS, PAGES 106–107: *Lost Highway* tour, Punchestown Racecourse, Dublin, Ireland, June 7, 2008. OPPOSITE: *Lost Highway* tour, soundcheck, Madison Square Garden, New York, NY, July 14, 2008. FOLLOWING, PAGE 110: *Lost Highway* tour, XCEL Energy Center, St. Paul, MN, March 2008; PAGE 111: *Lost Highway* tour, Great Lawn, Central Park, New York, NY, July 12, 2008; PAGES 112–113: *Crush* showcase concert, House of Blues, Chicago, IL, May 5, 2000.

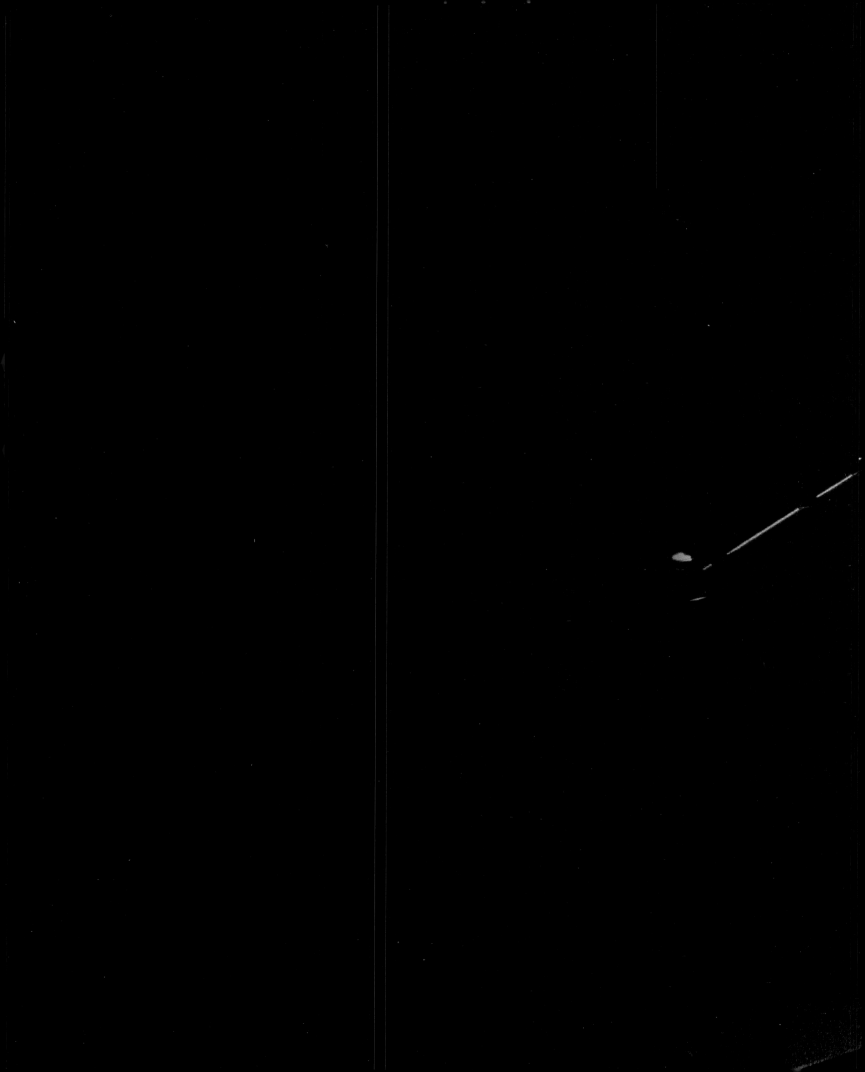

THE
SHOW

TICO: Emotions are what make a great song. It's one thing to write it, but if you can play it because you believe it and you feel it, that's special. I think people feel an honesty and purity in our music. You can't fabricate that. The message is in the relationships—between the band and our fans. And it's shared through the works—our songs, our live shows.

JON: People say, "Do you like playing stadium shows? I don't want to go out in front of stadiums. I want to be in an intimate club." Fuck that! I want to play the desert. And sell it out. More than once.

RICHIE: I think our fans get to exorcise their pains through the music we write. There is comfort in knowing they're not alone. They're feeling the gravity of the lyrics and it's accessible in their lives. When you go through something and someone else is feeling the same way you are, that's magic. When I was listening to "Layla," I knew Clapton was pining for Pattie Boyd. I was fourteen years old. I was pining for some chick myself at the time. I felt, "Hey, I'm not alone."

WHEN I'M UP THERE
I'M NOT THINKING ABOUT
THE LYRICS. I'M THINKING
"WHERE DO I TAKE
THIS CROWD?"
—JON

TICO: I've heard the most amazing things. People relate to the lyrics. Fans have cried over these songs. They'll say, "This song brought me through a very bad time in my life when I was sick." People actually thank you. That's pretty heavy—that your music can move people. There are certain songs that fans call their own.

JON: You've got to find things that last. Those songs touched people. They want to be a part of it. If they feel that, that's the thread of optimism in our music that helps them hold on in their lives. You can't just go out onstage and say, "Everything is right and bright." You can't do that; it'd be a lie.

TICO: I don't think we're here to preach. We're just as human as anybody else. We're real. We could stand on the soapbox and say we'll lead you through the waters, but that's bullshit.

PREVIOUS, PAGES 114–115: *Lost Highway* tour, Twickenham Stadium, London, England, June 28, 2008; PAGE 116: 6th Annual Charity Christmas Concert, backstage, Count Basie Theater, Red Bank, NJ, December 21, 1995; PAGES 116–117: *Lost Highway* tour, backstage pre-show huddle, XCEL Energy Center, St. Paul, MN, March 2008. THIS PAGE AND FOLLOWING, PAGES 120–121: *Lost Highway* tour, Punchestown Racecourse, Dublin, Ireland, June 7, 2008.

JON, IN MY OPINION, ON ANY GIVEN NIGHT, IS THE BEST FRONT MAN IN THE BUSINESS. —RICHIE

JON: The *These Days* record is perceived as being socially conscious or darker. "Hey God" and those kinds of songs worked great for me but they aren't necessarily the ones that work best live or became the ones I perform every night. Usually it's the songs like "It's My Life" and "Livin' On A Prayer" that say to those folks, "Come on, get up, you can do it! Get out there and fight the next round."

They're the ones that resonate. I know it's not easy for anybody in this day and age. It's getting harder every day.

People want optimism. They want to know that everything is going to be alright.

It's a sense of community: our community, each of us as individuals, our friends and families, the road crew, the record label staff, and the fans. We feel it.

JON: When I'm performing onstage, there is no character to hide behind. I don't put on another persona for that. It's all me. There's no "in and out of character." That's all there is. It's as me as me can get.

When I'm up there singing, I'm not thinking about the lyrics. I'm thinking about "What's the next song? What do I want to do?" I'm already past the moment. I'm looking back at it. I'm thinking, "Where am I gonna take this ride?"

During the breaks between songs, I'm like a boxer in his corner, thinking about what he's gonna do next and catching his breath.

The band are so consistent every night; my monitors are so consistent. I know if I'm singing great. I'm not worried about anything. It's just: "Where do I take this crowd?" They'll go with me if I take them to a quiet place. They'll listen to a slower song. They'll really listen to the words.

You have to find that compromise where you give them what they want and you give yourself what you need.

TICO: There are tides in all shows, in all songs. I don't think anybody wants to be going crazy the entire show. There are ups and downs, ebbs and flows.

JON: I love singing the older songs. Every one in the set I want to sing, still. I love the majesty of "Livin' On A Prayer." I know when we start that song, that crowd is gonna rise, and I'm gonna rise. I enjoy the tease of "Bad Name." I enjoy the exuberance of "It's My Life." I enjoy the cowboy imagery of "Wanted." I like all that. If I didn't enjoy a song, I wouldn't include it in the set list; I wouldn't sing it.

TICO: I could never go on idle—on cruise control—and play the show. It's impossible for me. You really have to give it your all. Plus, there are some audiences that react better and some that you really have to work at because of language or cultural differences.

PREVIOUS, PAGES 128–129: *Lost Highway* tour, Punchestown
Racecourse, Dublin, Ireland, June 7, 2008. THIS PAGE: *Lost
Highway* tour, XCEL Energy Center, St. Paul, MN, March 2008.
OPPOSITE: *Lost Highway* tour, Zentralstadion, Leipzig, Germany,
May 25, 2008. FOLLOWING, PAGE 133: *Lost Highway* tour,
City of Manchester Stadium, Manchester, England, June 22, 2008;
PAGES 134–135: *Lost Highway* tour, XCEL Energy Center, St.
Paul, MN, March 2008.

I WANT TO LIVE
IN THE MOMENT ONSTAGE
EVERY NIGHT.
—RICHIE

JON: Sometimes you have a night like Dublin, where it's pure magic. I love Ireland. I wish I was Irish. Somewhere in my past life, I was Irish. I know I was. I feel a connection. It isn't the architecture. It isn't the food. It's the people. I told my wife I'm jealous all the time because she and my kids are part Irish. I want to be adopted. I think every time I go to Ireland, the Irish fans know that.

I started flipping songs around in the Dublin set list midshow. I could add "Hallelujah." During "Hallelujah" I was in my own world entirely. Every audience is different. The Irish crowd wants lyrical content. Maybe it has to do with being able to speak in a common language. It's more about the lyrical connection than getting the whole audience to sway together or jump around.

Dublin expects greatness. They don't accept any nonsense. It's always a great crowd. They love us as much as we love them.

TICO: You can't take it for granted. It's special to be out here doing this. Once you take that for granted, you should just go home and do something else.

RICHIE: Who doesn't want my job? It's so fulfilling to walk out onstage and be confident in my performance, knowing I am going to deliver my soul to those people. I am completely at home and at peace up there.

I always try to get out of my body, spiritually, when I'm playing. I used to smoke to get high to help me get 'out there', but I realized that playing a guitar solo took me to that same place.

I'm striving for technical virtuosity and a spiritual virtuosity when I play because that's the way I grew up. When Hendrix was playing or B.B. King would play, Stevie Ray, Johnny Winter, Jimmy Page, Jeff Beck, Duane Allman, all those guys … it was spiritual.

The heart of this band is that we're good musicians. We ain't here by accident. We're proud to be a bunch of guys who pour their heart out every night. It's not inconsistent. This is every night. There's not a bad fucking show, ever.

The vocal game is so daunting from a physical standpoint: remaining healthy, keeping your voice in shape so you can get out there and sing and entertain a crowd and actually enjoy yourself without the nagging worry of wanting to hit a note and not being able to nail it. Physically, you're tired. If you haven't been taking care of your throat, you're a dead man.

Jon hasn't really had those problems since the *Jersey* era. He's been a tough, strong man and he's learned how to take care of himself and manage his voice, his instrument.

What's interesting for me has been watching Jon perform, especially over the last two tours. He's reached a place as a vocalist where he's unbelievable. Honest to God, Jon blows me away every night. He'll do something that he's never done in the twenty-five years we've been playing together and blow my mind.

TICO: We play our asses off but it really comes down to the front man. Jon is a great front man. He will get an audience up on their feet. He'll demand it of them. Jon's determined to get their asses up out of their seats, every last one of them, all the way up in the rafters. And they love to sing with the band. You could just stand there and play the music, but if you go that extra mile and make the crowd a part of the show there's nothing better. I want to look out from the stage and see you being goofy and dancing and singing. Jon's able to get thousands of people to do that.

RICHIE: I'm completely challenged by Jon onstage—still. It's not boring. I think that's part of what keeps our dynamic together. Of course there's me and I'm never boring, so he's always challenged, for different reasons maybe but, emotionally, he knows and I know that when I walk out onstage, my heart becomes that much bigger. When I walk out onstage, it's a part of my life that I love and feel comfortable with. It's like taking your clothes off in front of seventy thousand people every night.

We walk out there, even if we're tired or we're feeling like shit or something's happening in our personal life that isn't so great.

JON: We're all having fun but we're dead on when it comes to performing. We want be great on that stage, not some 80s rock cliché. The guys are all great players. I don't have to worry about them onstage.

RICHIE: Jon being a very handsome guy, I think our shows involve a lot of idol worship. It's like Elvis. We have a bit of that with Jon. Jon is that idol.

JON: Ours was the number one grossing tour in the world for 2008. Makes you feel good for a moment, but in the grand scheme it doesn't mean a thing. Numbers never meant fuckall to me. I don't need the applause. The applause is bullshit. I don't want a plaque. I just want to do the right thing …

I want to look out from the stage and watch people smile. I saw a girl with seriously debilitating MS out in the front row five concerts in a row. What this poor girl has got to go through to be in the front row. Just seeing her and the other eighty thousand healthy people out there and putting a smile on their faces, having that shared experience. That's what it's about.

RICHIE: We'd be assholes if we didn't appreciate every moment onstage because there are not many people who have the absolute privilege to actually walk out there and entertain that mass of humanity. And for us, it happens a lot. But it is exhausting.

JON: You commit to X amount of dates and you go out on tour and you do it well. I would never go out there and do an hour-and-a-half show. You can't. If I don't do two, two and a half, I feel unfulfilled. I get mad. We had one night on this last European tour where we did an hour fifty-five. The fan base knew it. I knew it. The band knew it.

I still toil over the set list, even on show number ninety-two into the tour. I still change it even in the midst of the show, juggle songs around. You don't want anyone to leave there with anything left in them—not the band, not the audience. Then you go home and your ears are ringing and your muscles are hurting and you lay down and you fall asleep thinking, "That's why I wanted to do this when I was a kid." You didn't cheat yourself, the fans, the dream, the promise, or the reality. You close your eyes and say, "You left it all out there—every bit of what you had."

BACKSTAGE

JON: It's crazy how you're dead tired and you get it together for showtime.

You're a mess. You'll wake up in the morning, you'll feel good for a while, and then around five o'clock, your body is gonna kill you. But you'll rise to the occasion again once you hit that concert stage. I'm experienced enough now to know it's OK. It's the physical part of my touring cycle. I don't worry about it now.

But an inexperienced kid is driving to a stadium show at five o'clock going, "Oh, my God, I'm so tired. What I need is the steroids. What I need is speed. What I need is alcohol. What I need is somebody to pat me on the back and tell me some bullshit."

The experienced guy says, "It's OK. It's five o'clock. Don't worry about it. Eight o'clock is coming. Don't touch the steroids. Don't touch the adrenaline. Don't need the caffeine." Then there it is, as always. Eight o'clock, I get up like I know I'm going into the ring.

The fuckin' steroids for my vocal chords are always in my bag. In my head I go, "Take it. Take it.

Take it." 'Cause part of me is saying, "Your chords are shot. You're tired. You can't make it through the show. You need them. Take them. Take them." It's fear and insecurity fueled by all the adrenaline.

My brain overpowers my body though and says, "Don't do it. You don't need it. You're fine." If I take the junk I'll go home, lay my head on my pillow, and say to myself, "You fucking failed." You pay the price for taking the junk—physically and mentally. I didn't take the junk. I didn't hit it at all this tour.

These days, towards the end of a tour, it's not my brain; it's my body that says no more, you're shutting down, to hell with your brain. Complete shutdown. We're gonna restart the computer. Don't worry right now; we're just rebooting.

PREVIOUS, PAGES 136–137: *One Wild Night* tour, pre-show chiropractic adjustment, backstage, San Jose Arena, San Jose, CA, April 23, 2001. OPPOSITE: The Shoe Inn, Middletown, NJ, December 10, 1999. FOLLOWING, PAGES 140–141: (ALL) *Lost Highway* tour, signing merchandise backstage pre-show, XCEL Energy Center, St. Paul, MN, March 2008.

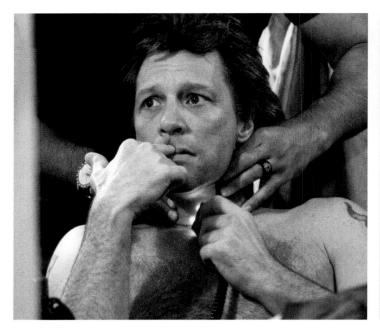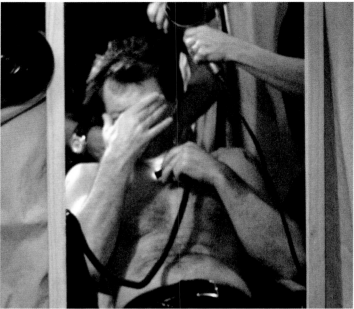

JON: Before every show, I warm up my vocal chords. But after the show, I cool down. Every night. Twenty years. Simple as that.

Around 1990, I was having a lot of problems with my voice. Little Steven said, "Katie Agresta." I called Katie and she asked me if I warmed down, and I said I'd never heard of such a thing. Then she asked me, "If you ran a marathon, would you go right to bed or would you walk it off?" I said, "You have my undivided attention."

For years, I'd visit her studio to sing, listen, learn. I'd bring Katie on the road whenever I felt beat up. I've relied on a cassette tape of her warm-down exercises from the day I met her. It's a religion. I take it with me everywhere. Ninety-nine percent of the time I won't go home from a show without it. U2 came to see us one night and after the show Bono asked, "How the hell do you run around and sing like that for two-and-a-half hours?" I told him what I tell everyone.

I warm up before the show. I warm down after the show. And I've got a chiropractor on the road. It all keeps me in real good shape.

Your vocal chords are as big as your thumbnail—for real. Those vocal warm-down exercises are a saving grace because if you don't sing well at night, you feel like a schmuck. Worst case scenario, you have to cancel the show and you don't want to disappoint fifty thousand people, the band, road crew …

The Dublin show was one of those days—it happens in those dusty green soccer fields—when my hay fever and allergies kicked in. I was in such pain. My eyes were swelling shut. I was sneezing like crazy. In my quick-change room, I was blowing my nose during every guitar solo. There's this thing in the back of your mouth, your soft palate. If you press on it with your tongue, fuck!!! You see stars and start sneezing and wheezing. I'm doing that between songs, looking at the boogers in my towel going, "Wow, that's disgusting!" I just keep blowing the snot out. The wardrobe girl's underneath the stage holding up a Sudafed and I'm motioning for her to put the tablets on my tongue during the show.

The show finally ramped up 'cause the Sudafed kicked in.

THIS PAGE: (BOTH) *Lost Highway* tour, mid-concert in quick-change tent, Twickenham Stadium, London, England, June 28, 2008. OPPOSITE: (ALL) *Lost Highway* tour, backstage pre-show, XCEL Energy Center, St. Paul, MN, March 2008. FOLLOWING, PAGE 144, LEFT: *One Wild Night* tour, Richie during pre-show warm-ups, San Jose Arena, San Jose, CA, April 23, 2001; RIGHT: *One Wild Night* tour, Jon during pre-show warm-ups, San Jose Arena, San Jose, CA, April 23, 2001; PAGE 145, TOP: Cool-down, post-radio station promo performance, San Francisco, CA, April 22, 2001; BOTTOM: *One Wild Night* tour, load in and stage build, March 2001.

JON: When you walk offstage, you're a loon. You're wired. You're shaking and pouring things on yourself. You've got that "momma strength" that could flip a car if it fell on your kid. It's an amazing amount of adrenaline surging through you.

I like the arena aspect of touring in America. You stay after, warm down, take a shower, have a glass of wine and a bite to eat. The band talks. Everybody gets their moment to say what went right, what went wrong. You see your guests and you leave an hour later.

In Europe, you do a runner. You race into the car. You're stinky and sweaty. You don't see the other guys and you speed away with police escorts. I hate the car trips. Some of the drives are so long. But you can't do it any other way at a stadium. You'd be stuck on-site for hours.

RICHIE: After the show, it's a natural wind down. Normally, we gather for a little food and just kind of bring each other down that way. Then you sit in your hotel room until your ears stop ringing. After all these years, I'm half deaf. It's an occupational hazard. I think I'm probably deafer than anybody in the band.

JON: You give everything and then some. You sacrifice. I miss out on some of the self-indulgence. I don't have as many personal days.

In London, Richie hung with Jimmy Page, spent the whole day and night with his hero. Tico realized the dream of launching Rock Star Baby at Harrods with his son and wife by his side. Dave attended Wimbledon with his girlfriend and sat center court. I sat in my hotel room working on football business.

WE EARNED THE RIGHT TO WEAR ONE OF THESE. THIS IS SOMETHING WE SHARED TOGETHER.
—JON

JON: We gave out the first batch of medallions in 1987 in the Madison Square Garden backstage hallway during the *Slippery When Wet* tour. I'd had a dozen made for the band and management. I thought, at that time, if it all ended then and there, I'd give everybody a little something to remember just how big the *Slippery* tour was.

The pendant was in the shape of the Superman logo, like my little tattoo, with the Slippery When Wet road sign inside. It's gold and diamonds. They're not inscribed. The original model is what it is and has never been improved upon. They're made by a little secret guy in New York. You really can't get one.

People would ask me about it and I'd explain it was similar to Elvis's TCB [Taking Care of Business]. People want them. They'd ask, "Can I have one?" No! We earned the right to wear one of these. This is something that we shared together. The man who taught me to play the guitar—I put mine in his coffin. I never got a replacement. Mine's gone.

You have to do at least two world tours start to finish before you get one. And each tour, ten, fifteen, twenty people qualify because they work with us tour after tour. We won't see crew members for a year or two, but you go watch somebody else's concert, they'll be working that tour and they'll be wearing our medallion. It's sort of a wink and a nod. People know who they worked for.

I'd say there are maybe one hundred medallions out there in the world and they were earned. People—I think, I hope—are pretty proud to earn one, because it really means that we've been through a lot together.

JON: You've got to remember all of these gifts and opportunities came from so much fucking work, every single day. We're where we are now in our lives and our careers because we worked to get here.

Life on the road is no vacation. Unfortunately, I don't get to see the world. What I see is hotel rooms, the gym, the restaurant, the bar, the airport. It's a shame, but I'm never anywhere long enough and you can't. I see very, very little because you don't have days off. You've got 130 guys and twenty-seven trucks. You can't keep everyone sitting around so you can sightsee.

I try to grab some pictures on occasion. It's nice when I look back and see the photos of us in Jakarta, the pictures in India. I've been to India three times, but I haven't really seen anything unless you count doing a photo session in the street.

How psychotic is it to sit in an empty dressing room, then go out onto a stage with seventy thousand screaming maniacs, only to get back in the car where there's total silence, and then go back to a hotel room and sit there all by yourself? I just got off this massive stage and that's all there is. Ringing. That'll fuck you up.

RICHIE: I feel better and younger than I've felt in a long, long time now. I'm also more enriched by this life and it feels much fuller to me. I'm much more present, these days. I want to live in the moment onstage every night.

PREVIOUS, PAGE 146, TOP: *Lost Highway* tour, post-show return to dressing room, XCEL Energy Center, St. Paul, MN, March 2008; BOTTOM: Soundcheck, San Jose Arena, San Jose, CA, April 23, 2001; PAGE 147, TOP: *Lost Highway* tour, Richie Sambora's guitar rack under the stage, 2008; BOTTOM: *Lost Highway* tour, backstage images, XCEL Energy Center, St. Paul, MN, March 2008; PAGE 149: (ALL) *Lost Highway* tour, pre-show "Class of 2008" pendant ceremony, backstage hallway, Madison Square Garden, New York, NY, July 14, 2008. THIS PAGE: *Lost Highway* tour, Tico leaving the stage, Punchestown Racecourse, Dublin, Ireland, June 7, 2008. OPPOSITE: Jon in a local pub, Marbella, Spain, June 2008. FOLLOWING, PAGES 152–153: Press and promo day for *Bounce* album, Sterling Sound, New York, NY, July 23, 2002.

TICO: Life on the road is not normal. As much as we're a family, as much as you reach out to the people around you, you've still got a sheet of paper slipped under your hotel room door every night that tells you what you're doing the next day and where and when you have to do it. It's not a natural way of living. You are eating from room service. You can't even make your own coffee. They're the little things I want when I go home. They are the simple things that most people want to get away from. Personally, I want to be able to do those things for myself.

JON: You know, I go out there like a prizefighter and answer the bell every night. But when I get done with a tour, God, I'm tired. I look in the mirror and say, "Whoa, you've aged this year."

I hope I'm able to just turn it off without breaking down. This dates back twenty years and other guys in my peer group will attest. You're on the road, the tour ends, and then you go home. You're a dead man the next day. You're obviously jetlagged, exhausted from the shows, and your body shuts down. But come nine o'clock, your pulse will rise. Your heartbeat will race. It's showtime … and there's no show.

RICHIE: There isn't any real come down period. You take a couple a weeks off and you get the kids and you've got to go on vacation.

JON: I go home and introduce myself to my family again. 'Cause it's a very selfish place, me doing this. There are four kids at home going, "Where were you?"

RICHIE: We spend more time together than with our own families sometimes. The challenge is when you get home, trying to be really, really present.

BEYOND THE BAND

To me, any artist needs to find fuel wherever he can—reading different books, seeing different movies and plays, whatever it is that inspires you. I absolutely encourage everyone to go and find different circles of friends simply because, when we get together, we've got something else to talk about.

The Arena Football League is all about community, family, access, and affordability. Those values define the Philadelphia Soul, the team I co-own; we are one of the premiere teams in the AFL and Arena Bowl XXII Champions.

Giving back to your community isn't done enough in professional sports. It's all about me, me, me. From the day we launched the Soul franchise, I had a vision of using the team as a launching pad for helping the Philadelphia community. Everything we do has a charitable angle. Dedication to community service has been the cornerstone of our franchise.

I'd been reading a bunch of American history books. I was staying in Philadelphia and looked out the window of my gilded cage. It was a cold, snowy night and I saw a man sleeping on the steps of city hall in Philadelphia, the birthplace of our nation. The man was freezing on the street in the dead of winter. I didn't believe that was what Jefferson and Franklin and Adams and Washington had envisioned.

I called Obie O'Brien, the band's engineer and my dear friend, up to my room at two A.M. I said, "I got an idea." I gave him a mission: Find the person who will help me fix this. And he found me Sister Mary Scullion.

She's a Sister of Mercy. She doesn't wear a habit. She curses and she spits. She calls it as she sees it and she don't take any guff from anybody.

Sister Mary's been my mentor, adhering to the age-old adage about giving a man a fish versus teaching him to fish on his own.

She founded Project H.O.M.E. [Housing, Opportunities for Employment, Medical Care, Education] in Philadelphia and has addressed every component of homelessness, from drug addiction and alcoholism to mental illness. She's ushered people, literally, from the alleyways, through rehab, and all the way to affordable rentals and permanent housing.

Project H.O.M.E. offers job training and provides services to the community, and it helps rebuild those neighborhoods, bringing pride back to those places. You meet so many people who are so warm, wonderful, loving, caring, hardworking, and determined. Opportunities just didn't knock on their doors the same way they did for others.

That first time I met Sister Mary she said something that was quite moving but really threw me off. She said, "I've been waiting for you."

"Me?" I think it was just someone like me.

We created a real bond and we've done great things together. We've been able to expose Sister Mary and Project H.O.M.E. to a broader audience while putting the issue of homelessness in the spotlight.

The Philadelphia Soul Charitable Foundation was founded as the natural extension of the football team's philanthropic priorities. The Foundation's mission is to help stem the cycle of poverty that leads to homelessness.

That's what the Philadelphia Soul Charitable Foundation's stood for now for three official years, and five years since we launched the team.

We work with partners and organizations to reach our goals. Government dollars are good but it takes private equity and, more importantly, homeowners and others in the neighborhood to rally around the effort. I can easily see the vision. I can help bring these parties together and, hopefully, reform and rebuild communities and neighborhoods.

Every charity is a good charity so long as it's really getting to the bottom line. But in light of what's happened in America in the last few years, our dedication to ending poverty and homelessness truly, and unfortunately, placed us ahead of the curve.

So far, we've built a total of 140 homes—including some exclusively for veterans—with Project H.O.M.E. We broke ground in Newark, New Jersey, at a site for fifty permanent rentals through a partnership with HELP USA. We've expanded beyond the Philadelphia/New Jersey region; we've had a hand in building homes now in Louisiana, Detroit, Atlanta, LA, Colorado, Brooklyn, and even South Africa.

Now we're confident and experienced. I feel a great sense of pride. I'm still learning, mind you. I'm not a novice anymore—just barely above that level. But I can speak on the subject with passion. You learn so much every day. It's all working right now. We have experience, we have desire, we're committed, and we're not getting too big too soon. I feel very proud. If people could only understand how good we feel when we see a family in their new home. I wish everyone could experience that same euphoria we've felt.

My music and my philanthropic work are two different worlds. I don't feel the need to preach about what the Foundation does from the concert stage nor do I feel the need to talk about my music and concerts during a site dedication or groundbreaking. Keep them separate: two different aspects of the same life. And they're both fulfilling.

I just feel the need to be a more well-rounded person, to stop suffering from LSD—lead singer's disease: me, me, me, me, me. That's a shallow existence.

After the first of two Detroit concerts, I went to my room, went to bed, did all the right things. It was exciting to wake up early, put on a nice shirt, shave, and attend a press conference, break ground, dedicate a house we had a hand in building. To me, that's the greatest thing about the Foundation's work. You get more out of giving back than you do in receiving. It's a lot of work but it's all about the end result, what you believe will be something better.

You can't always just take; you gotta give. That's the law of the universe.

I found a cause, a reason, something that was nondenominational. There were no prejudices involved. Doesn't matter if you're black, white, young, old, Republican, Democrat. Homelessness is something that can potentially affect anyone. You can relate to it whether you live in Germany, Paris, Tokyo, or Philadelphia.

Sometimes you get so caught up in the day-to-day that you're not aware beyond your own life. That's normal. But what is it that motivates and moves you? People just have to find "it" and they'll get involved and make a difference in the lives of others. That person could be the next community leader. Who knows? We change the world, one person at a time. One state. One city. One neighborhood. One block. One home. One family. One soul at a time.

Nothing wrong with that romantic vision of what the country can and should be.

THE FACT THAT YOU CAN EXPLORE
DIFFERENT ELEMENTS BESIDES MUSIC
IS VERY IMPORTANT.
—TICO

TICO: I've been an artist since I was five. As an only child, I had a lot of time alone where I would paint and create. Music took grip of me when I was eleven or twelve and I was unstoppable. Art was put off to the side while I played music, which provided more immediate feedback and gratification.

In the early 90s, I saw an art store and said, "I'm going back to this." I built a studio in SoHo and locked myself in there for months and months and months at a time.

I got lost in there. All I did was work. Wore clogs and paint clothes. I looked like I was sick. I weighed 130 pounds. Sometimes I'd just forget to eat. Before I knew it, I had several hundred pieces done.

There have been times we've had a couple years off between albums and tours so I'd get lost in my art. I had to be creative. It's the way I grew up and everything that's creative is good for me. It's good energy. The fact that you can explore different elements besides music is very important.

When I found art again it gave me a chance to be spiritual by myself. You get creative making records but when you're on tour, you're not all that creative. Every night you're playing. Art was something where I didn't need anybody else. I needed to do it on my own.

When you're creating with other musicians, it's the interaction that combines into one entity, which is special. But being able to go inside yourself, on your own and pull something creative out ... it fulfills me.

And, spiritually, it got everything out of me, whether it was love, anger, whatever I wanted. And I couldn't be arrested for it!

I'm a musician. I'm an artist. That's just part of who I am. There is no doubt I could have survived without being in this band and made a living as an artist. But I think the art made me a better person, a better creator, a better musician ... because music is just painting with sound instead of colors. It's intertwined. Art gave me

another outlet to be creative, something I could do for the rest of my life, which I really love and enjoy. And being in the financial situation with Bon Jovi, I never have to starve being an artist. I already did that as a musician. I remember those nineteen-cent boxes of macaroni and cheese.

Rock Star Baby is another big endeavor for me. When the first of the guys in the band were having kids, we wanted to buy cool stuff for the babies and there just wasn't anything cool. That inspired my brainchild, the Rock Star Baby line. Now we have children's clothing, jewelry, strollers, cosmetics, home decor, you name it.

That's what I do on my days off (if I'm not golfing!). I'm on e-mail. I'm on the phone. It's creating a lifestyle for the family that wants to be hipper.

DAVID: When you work on your own art and nobody else is with you, you grow individually. You get better at being yourself and that makes it that much better when the band all regroup. We can be better at our craft with more life under our belt.

In 1999 I got together with Francine Pascal who at the time had Sweet Valley High, a book series. We worked on a rock 'n' roll stage version of the Sweet Valley High book series.

Then right at the end of 2001, I read the script of *Memphis*. I could hear the finished product in my head. I knew what it was. It told the story of the first white DJ to put black music on the radio. It was fictionalized but based on real characters.

Joe DiPietro, the creator, said he'd waited to find the right collaborator because it's a story about music and the birth of rock 'n' roll. He needed a real rock 'n' roll guy, not a theater guy who thought he could rock. Joe allowed me into that world. The lines are blurred. We're really partners.

In Bon Jovi, in the band, I play a part. It's Jon's vision and we back him up and then add our parts to that vision—our vision within his vision. But in the theater world, it's my vision.

When you're the composer, it's pretty cool having everybody sit in the room and look to you. There's a nine-piece band and twenty-six actors. I wrote every note that comes out of everybody's mouth and every note that every instrument plays, and I cowrote all the lyrics.

It's a really complicated art form. It's acting; it's singing; it's dancing—and doing it all live. You have to put it up and try to fix it. It's like problem solving and I really love that. I'll be sleepless until I solve the puzzle.

It's good fortune how everything is colliding. Both *The Toxic Avenger* and *Memphis* are Broadway bound. But the band has to tour. That's my main gig, for now, and I love it. Eventually, I'll have to figure out how to coexist in the theater and rock 'n' roll worlds.

WE CAN BE BETTER AT OUR CRAFT WITH MORE LIFE UNDER OUR BELT. —DAVID

SOLO ENDEAVORS AND PERSONAL PROJECTS HAVE BEEN AN IMPORTANT PART OF THIS BAND'S GROWTH.
—RICHIE

RICHIE: Independent pursuits keep you strong and confident. We have to learn and grow and be inspired and moved. We have to be individuals so we can be a stronger group. It's paramount in our success equation. Individually everybody has their own projects that are enriching to their own spirits. That's very important stuff. I am dying to do a solo record again. I love making records, beyond the band, just working with other artists. I love to get called for sessions and do movie soundtracks and branch out.

Working with other producers and other great musicians, you are always learning. There is always a great interchange of "I'll teach you this. You teach me that." It's part of the ongoing education process that makes this organization work. You bring back new information and new ideas to the band. Even if it's a small thing, a slight educational process you went through, it's all good. It makes the whole stronger when the individual parts are stronger and more creative and more inspired.

My talent, my own education process, my own commitment to learning means I'm open to everything.

I could do a solo record wherever I wanted and whenever I wanted with whomever I wanted.

I always approached my solo albums with a lot more artistic freedom because no one is expecting anything of me except a fresh look, a fresh musical painting. I'd get the best musicians I know, people with whom I'd always wanted to work, always wanted to co-produce, and not care about the finances really. When you do a solo album, the learning experience is that much more intense. Every day you walk into the studio and wear a dozen different hats. You're the songwriter, the guitar player, the lead singer, the background singer, the arranger, and the co-producer. So you're really juggling a lot of responsibilities. I can't wait to do another one.

JON: I'm really rooted right now, just on that steady course, knowing who I am, what I am, and where I'm going. So it's nice, maybe, to watch my bandmates blossom.

25 YEARS

JON: We're not supposed to still be here. When you played your first block dance in Sayreville, you thought that was the big time. Subsequently, the club in Asbury to getting a record deal you thought was the big time; to headlining the first time, you thought was the big time; to when *Slippery* came out, you thought, "It can't get bigger than *Slippery*." Then when you look back, you go, "Oh, no, no, no, no." The subsequent tours were so much bigger. You never really run out of what is the big time.

In today's world, it would be very hard to break like we did. Then again, with YouTube and MySpace and Facebook and Twitter, there are new avenues that kids are gonna go travel and they'll find their own way.

TICO: It helps to be very young. You go for it because you believe only in it. I think we had that notion like kids do now. They'll get where they want to go and find a way to do it.

DAVID: You really have to be a hard worker. You have to have an insane amount of drive.

JON: I'm sure there are great kid bands out there that could kick our ass but there's a difference between having a pop celebrity moment in time and having a career. Don't talk to me about one-, five-, or ten-year careers.

When you get to twenty years, to twenty-five, when you get to forty years and the songs have stood the test of time, then talk to me about a career, a legacy.

Leonard Cohen has a legacy. Paul Simon, Bob Dylan have a legacy. Among the pop kids today, there will be celebrities. They may even be icons, but to have been respected for influencing their generation and the generations that come after, that is the goal.

There was an eighteen-year-old kid from Lebanon who came to our shows. Why is he into a forty-six-year-old guy who's been making records longer than he's even been alive? Why were we the biggest show ever held in Abu Dhabi? We didn't have a hit record there. It's the body of work. It's the history onstage. It's the impact that we've made across generations.

RICHIE: Some people think we're a new band. They just discovered us two albums ago. They have the opportunity, which is probably pretty interesting, to rediscover the older stuff.

JON: There's nothing like that feeling when music changes your life. When you get a chance to see or meet or open for someone you look up to and they like your music, they give you something indescribable. Southside Johnny was that person for me when I was a kid. It was pretty great stuff.

It's cool to talk to some of these bands that open for us. Every kid draws the same inspiration from somebody who came before. It's wonderful to be part of that line in history, traveling from the getting to giving end of it. It's just as rewarding.

RICHIE: There's a learning process. OK, where do you go now? Where's the next road, man? Where's the next path? It's an exciting thing for a musician.

We're always striving to do great work, to create something special. It would be no fun for us; there would be no reason to do it, if that wasn't a main part of the equation.

DAVID: We're completely past the point of ever saying, "Fuck you—I'm walking away from this." Now it's so much fun to walk onstage. But there's the reality check, knowing that the older you get and the longer this timeline goes, there's the chance you'll be doing it less and less.

PREVIOUS, PAGES 166–167: *Lost Highway* tour, XCEL Energy Center, St. Paul, MN, March 2008; PAGES 168–169: Band photo shoot, The Eleanor, Long Island City, NY, December 2, 2008. OPPOSITE: "Whole Lot of Leavin'" portrait session, Minneapolis, MN, March 17, 2008. FOLLOWING, PAGES 172–173: *Lost Highway* tour, Manchester, England, 2008; PAGE 174: Promotional portrait session, The Palace of Auburn Hills, Auburn Hills, MI, July 7, 2008; PAGES 176–177: *Lost Highway* tour, end of show, XCEL Energy Center, St. Paul, MN, March 2008.

RICHIE: People ask me what keeps us out there, what keeps us going. Number one, it's in my blood and I love to do it. If I wasn't getting paid I'd still be making music someplace. I'd be doing it anyway.

DAVID: We truly want the best for each other. We're there for each other. We're fortunate. We're a band of brothers. When one man falls, we're there to pick him up.

If the phone rang and any one of these guys was on the line and said help—it ain't about a record, it ain't about anything—the reply is "What do you need? What can I do for you?"

RICHIE: There aren't many things that we don't know about each other after all these years. There's really nothing to hide at this point.

JON: You're closer than you would be with your siblings. That's a fact. There's no question. We shared more of our lives. Half of our entire lives we've spent with each other.

RICHIE: One of the secrets to our success is that we've never tried to be anybody else or something we're not. But I think our continual forward motion is a great challenge.

DAVID: You don't have any guarantees. You can put out that next record and it could tank.

TICO: You're only as good as your last word, your last effort.

RICHIE: We don't take that for granted.

DAVID: Every time you put something out there, you step into the ring. You better have done your training. You better get ready to fight because you can get knocked out. There's no guarantee.

JON: It's OK to be afraid. It's OK to be excited. It's OK to laugh, cry, hurt, indulge, whatever. Reach outside your comfort zone. Do not get comfortable. Once you get too comfortable then you're on that slide and then it's nostalgia. Then you're taking pictures of the past.

RICHIE: Having such a big life in this band—it's big, man. This is a machine, an organism that encompasses you on an emotional level if you are going to bring that. For me, I bring it 100 percent every time I show up.

JON: There's only twenty-four hours in a day. Maybe the cost of all this is that I've spent too many nights sleeping in hotel rooms with a sleeping pill and a bottle of wine and missing my kid's school play.

Whatever I wanted to do artistically, whether it worked or didn't, I did it. There was never the fear of anything. There's no "if only." Very few regrets around here, man.

It's July and I'm at a crossroads emotionally and spiritually. I just can't pack up a suitcase and go again. I just can't. It'll be interesting to see where I go next year. The mind is starting to spin, but I'm cursing that guitar right now. I just don't wanna see it. I don't wanna talk to it. I don't want it to stare at me as I walk through the room. I wanna leave it lying there. Eventually, I'll tease it and it'll tease me and the circus will begin again. But it's a process, a tough process so you gotta be up for it.

RICHIE: Jon and I will get together and start writing again. We'll start stockpiling for the next installment of what Bon Jovi is going to look like. That's the exciting part, seeing where we go next.

JON: Twenty-five years in the history … and I'm still in the process …

PAGE 2: *Lost Highway* tour, end of show, XCEL Energy Center, St. Paul, MN, March 2008. PAGE 4: "Whole Lot of Leavin'" portrait session, Minneapolis, MN, March 17, 2008. PAGE 6: *Lost Highway* tour, Richie Sambora's guitar rack, 2008. PAGES 8-9: *Lost Highway* tour set lists, denoting which guitars Richie needs for which show, 2008.

CREDITS

MANY THANKS TO ILENE SCHREIBMAN,

EDITORIAL AND ARCHIVAL CONSULTANT,

AND TO THE PHOTOGRAPHERS WHO

CONTRIBUTED PHOTOS TO THIS BOOK.

PHOTOGRAPHS

UNLESS OTHERWISE NOTED, ALL PHIL GRIFFIN PHOTOGRAPHS
WERE TAKEN IN 2008.

2: Phil Griffin

4: Phil Griffin

6: Phil Griffin

8–9: Phil Griffin

10–11: Phil Griffin

13: Phil Griffin

14–15: Phil Griffin

16–17: Kevin Westenberg

18–19: Phil Griffin (all)

PREVIOUS, PAGE 179: Contact sheet of outtakes from *One Wild Night: Live 1984–2001* photo shoot, 5th and Sunset, Los Angeles, CA, March 19, 2001. THIS PAGE: *Lost Highway* tour, XCEL Energy Center, St. Paul, MN, March 2008.

20–21: Phil Griffin

22–23: Herbie Knott/Rex

24–25: Phil Griffin

26–27: Phil Griffin (2009)

29: photos from the personal collections of Tico Torres,

Jon Bon Jovi, and Richie Sambora

30: from the personal collection of Jon Bon Jovi

(top and bottom); Mark "WEISSGUY" Weiss/

www.markweiss.com (center)

32: Mark "WEISSGUY" Weiss/www.markweiss.com

33: Mark "WEISSGUY" Weiss/www.markweiss.com

34: from the personal collection of Jon Bon Jovi (top);

Mark "WEISSGUY" Weiss/www.markweiss.com

(center and bottom)

34–35: Mark "WEISSGUY" Weiss/www.markweiss.com

36–37: Phil Griffin

39: Mark "WEISSGUY" Weiss/www.markweiss.com

40–41: Mark "WEISSGUY" Weiss/www.markweiss.com

42–43: Phil Griffin (2009)

44: Mark "WEISSGUY" Weiss/www.markweiss.com

45: Sam Erickson

46: Mark "WEISSGUY" Weiss/www.markweiss.com (left),

Guido Karp (right)

47: Mark "WEISSGUY" Weiss/www.markweiss.com

48–49: Mark "WEISSGUY" Weiss/www.markweiss.com

(all)

50: Phil Griffin

53: Sam Erickson

54–55: Phil Griffin

56: Phil Griffin

58: Phil Griffin (2009)

60: Olaf Heine (all)

61: Olaf Heine

62–63: Phil Griffin

64: Mark "WEISSGUY" Weiss/www.markweiss.com

65: Mark "WEISSGUY" Weiss/www.markweiss.com (left),

Sam Erickson (right)

67: Phil Griffin (all); Frank Sinatra image @ William P.

Gottlieb; www.jazzphotos.com

68: Olaf Heine (all)

69: Sam Erickson

70: Olaf Heine (top), Cynthia Levine (bottom)

71: Olaf Heine

72: Phil Griffin

73: Phil Griffin

74–75: Phil Griffin

76: Sam Erickson

77: Phil Griffin

78–79: Mark "WEISSGUY" Weiss/www.markweiss.com

80–81: Neil Zlozower

82–83: Phil Griffin (2009)

85: Phil Griffin (2009)

86: Phil Griffin (2009)

87: Phil Griffin (2009)

88: Mark "WEISSGUY" Weiss/www.markweiss.com

89: Mark "WEISSGUY" Weiss/www.markweiss.com

90–91: Phil Griffin

92: Mark "WEISSGUY" Weiss/www.markweiss.com

93: Phil Griffin (2009)

94–95: Phil Griffin (2009)

95: Phil Griffin (2009)

96–97: Phil Griffin (2009)

98–99: Phil Griffin

100–101: Phil Griffin

102–103: Phil Griffin

104–105: Phil Griffin (all) (2009)

106–107: Phil Griffin

108: Phil Griffin

110: Phil Griffin

111: Phil Griffin

112–113: Mark "WEISSGUY" Weiss/www.markweiss.com

114–115: Phil Griffin

116: Mark "WEISSGUY" Weiss/www.markweiss.com

116–117: Phil Griffin

118–119: Phil Griffin

120–121: Phil Griffin

122–123: Phil Griffin

123: Phil Griffin (all)

124–125: Phil Griffin

126–127: composite of photos by Phil Griffin

128–129: Phil Griffin

130: Phil Griffin

131: Phil Griffin

133: Phil Griffin

134–135: Phil Griffin

136–137: Cynthia Levine

OPPOSITE, CLOCKWISE FROM TOP LEFT: Jon celebrating first gold record presentation with family, backstage, Brendan Byrne Arena, Meadowlands Sports Complex, East Rutherford, NJ, October 18, 1985; Jon and Richie during first Bon Jovi tour, 1984; Moscow Music Peace Festival, Lenin Stadium, Moscow, U.S.S.R., August 13, 1989; Jon and Richie with the guitar, signed by Bob Dylan, which Richie gave to Jon for his birthday, New York, NY, February 6, 2008; Richie working on New Jersey album at Little Mountain Recording Studios, Vancouver, B.C., Canada, Spring 1988; Crush showcase concert, House of Blues, Chicago, IL, May 5, 2000.

138: Olaf Heine

140: Olaf Heine (all)

141: Olaf Heine

142: Phil Griffin (all)

143: Phil Griffin (all)

144: Cynthia Levine (all)

145: Cynthia Levine (all)

146: Phil Griffin (top), Cynthia Levine (bottom)

147: Phil Griffin (all)

149: Phil Griffin (all)

150: Phil Griffin

151: Phil Griffin

152–153: Sam Erickson

154–155: Phil Griffin (all)

157: Olaf Heine

158: Phil Griffin (top), Harvey Finkle/www.harveyfinkle.com (center), Pete Byron (bottom)

160: Olaf Heine

161: from the personal collection of Tico Torres, postcard image by Dana Vitale

162: Olaf Heine

163: Phil Griffin

164: Olaf Heine

166–167: Phil Griffin

168-169: Phil Griffin

171: Phil Griffin

172-173: Phil Griffin

174: Phil Griffin

176-177: Phil Griffin

179: Marina Chavez

180: Phil Griffin

183: (clockwise from top left) from the personal collection of Jon Bon Jovi; from the personal collection of Richie Sambora; Mark "WEISSGUY"Weiss/www.markweiss.com; from the personal collection of Richie Sambora; from the personal collection of Jon Bon Jovi; Mark "WEISSGUY"Weiss/www.markweiss.com (center)

184: (clockwise from top left) from the personal collection of Jon Bon Jovi; Phil Griffin; from the personal collection of Richie Sambora; from the personal collection of Tico Torres; from the personal collection of Richie Sambora; from the personal collection of Richie Sambora; from the personal collection of David Bryan

187: Phil Griffin

OPPOSITE, CLOCKWISE FROM TOP LEFT: Jon and Dorothea, Seaside Heights, NJ, summer 1980; Tico and son, Hector, Jr., backstage, Madison Square Garden, New York, NY, July 14, 2008; Richie with parents, Adam and Joan Sambora, Teterboro Airport, Teterboro, NJ, 2005; Tico and son, Hector, Jr., RockStar Baby photo shoot; Richie and daughter, Ava, backstage, 2000; Richie and daughter, Ava, Los Angeles, 2005; David and family on holiday, St. Barts, 2008. FOLLOWING, PAGE 187: *Lost Highway* tour, XCEL Energy Center, St. Paul, MN, March 2008.

BON JOVI

WHEN WE WERE BEAUTIFUL

HarperCollins books may be purchased for educational, business, or sales promotional use. For information please write: Special Markets Department, HarperCollins*Publishers*, 10 East 53rd Street, New York, NY 10022.

First published in 2009 by
Collins Design
An Imprint of HarperCollins*Publishers*
10 East 53rd Street
New York, NY 10022
Tel: (212) 207-7000
Fax: (212) 207-7654
collinsdesign@harpercollins.com
www.harpercollins.com

Distributed throughout the world by
HarperCollins*Publishers*
10 East 53rd Street
New York, NY 10022
Fax: (212) 207-7654

Design by Agnieszka Stachowicz
Front cover photo by Phil Griffin

Library of Congress Control Number: 2009927516

ISBN 978-0-06-186415-5

Printed in the United States
First Printing, 2009